A.A. in Prison

INMATE to INMATE

Alcoholics Anonymous World Services, Inc., New York, N.Y.

A.A. IN PRISON: INMATE TO INMATE

Copyright © 1991 by
Alcoholics Anonymous World Services, Inc.

Mail address:
475 Riverside Drive
New York, NY 10115

First printing 1991
Twenty-seventh printing 2005

www.aa.org

*This is A.A. General Service
Conference-approved literature*

It was recommended that: The trustees' Correctional Facilities Committee recommendation for publication of a collection of correctional facilities stories from previous Grapevines (and other A.A. sources) be approved. (Advisory Action of the 40th General Service Conference.)

ISBN 0-916856-41-0

Printed in the United States of America

40M 10/05 (BP)   **B-13**

A.A. in Prison
INMATE to INMATE

Foreword

The stories in this book originally appeared in the A.A. Grapevine, A.A.'s international monthly magazine. They are the personal stories of the miracle of recovery as told by 32 inmates, who found freedom and hope from the devastating disease of alcoholism through the program of Alcoholics Anonymous. These A.A.s share their experience with you in the hope you will identify with their problem and gain the strength through the Twelve Steps, fellowship and tools of the A.A. program to join them on the road to recovery—physically, mentally and spiritually—from alcoholism.

I have seen hundreds of families set their feet in the path that really goes somewhere; have seen the most impossible domestic situations righted; feuds and bitterness of all sorts wiped out. I have seen men come out of asylums and resume a vital place in the lives of their families and communities. There is scarcely any form of trouble and misery which has not been overcome among us.

Co-founder, Bill W.
in "Bill's Story"
Alcoholics Anonymous, p. 15

Alcoholics Anonymous® is a fellowship of men and women who share their experience, strength and hope with each other that they may solve their common problem and help others to recover from alcoholism.

The only requirement for membership is a desire to stop drinking. There are no dues or fees for AA membership; we are self-supporting through our own contributions. AA is not allied with any sect, denomination, politics, organization or institution; does not wish to engage in any controversy, neither endorses nor opposes any causes. Our primary purpose is to stay sober and help other alcoholics to achieve sobriety.

Contents

*Indicates month and year that the story appeared in The A.A. Grapevine.

As a recent prisoner who found the A.A. program in prison and now a parolee attending outside meetings of Alcoholics Anonymous, I feel that my Janus-faced status between the past and the future puts me in a position to give the *ins-and-outs* of the program so that those outside may look within, and those inside may look out . . . with some assurance of remaining out once they are released.

So, right now, right here, I tell you that the place and time to begin working the A.A. program—whether you are in or out—is: right here, right now.

Many of you on the inside point to the "wheels" who were active in A.A. in prison, but who got off the bus, hit a bar and bounced back. "What's the use?" you argue. "This racket won't keep a guy out." You are so right . . . as a racket it won't keep us out of prison. But, as a program, it will.

There is more to the program than reading the Twelve Steps and making pitches for the benefit of the visiting A.A.s from the outside, then following the pitches with personal appeals for help in getting out. Unless your words go out from a sounding board that is your heart, enriched by sincerity and humility, you are no more on this program than a parrot, quoting Shakespeare, is erudite.

For three years I listened to men make pitches that dwelt on what they were going to do when they got out. That was the tenor of my own first few pitches. But I'm not a pie-in-the-sky guy. An old disciple of Omar Khayyam's, I held fast to the philosophy that it is better to take the cash and let the credit go. Most of us in prison have always operated on that principle because emotional immaturity does not grasp the abstract. So I dropped out of A.A. for about two months, using a night job as an excuse. But I had no excuse for not attending church on Sunday mornings. . . .

Both A.A. and church attendance look good on our records when we go up before the Parole Board. Both are yokes that rub the shoulders raw when our motive is to get out. Heaven seemed a million light years away, and I had the feeling I'd be a burned-out star before I crossed that much space. "What can I get out of it right now?" I fretted. The answer came slowly: the realm of values and morals is real.

But church hadn't solved my alcoholism, so I read the A.A. book, *Alcoholics Anonymous*, my eye on Chapter Five, "How It Works." I started back to A.A., this time not to get on the program when I got out, but to get whatever it had to offer me in prison. It was still cash-

and-carry with me—I didn't trust Bill or Dr. Bob's IOU deal.

That is how I hit on the *right here, right now* theme that began to color my pitches. I thought it was luck then; later, I knew that it was God as I understand Him. I got my pay every day. The first coin was the realization that emotional patterns caused me to seek escape in alcohol. That demanded an honest inventory, and A.A.'s moral inventory was the hardest step of all.

About that time I was selected as a guinea pig for psychotherapy, an innovation in the California Department of Corrections program. Thanks to A.A., I was completely honest with myself and my therapist. It took a whole year, but—little by little—A.A., my church and psychotherapy were revealed to me as interdependent and correlated approaches to a personality change.

I still don't know what happened to me. The hatred for prison officials was resentment that A.A. told me I couldn't afford. The psychotherapist showed me that officials were but scapegoats for my childhood frustrations by a harsh father. My church told me to forgive my enemies. I ended by silently asking *their* forgiveness. The change? Where I once had gloated over destroying state property (as a child, I would slyly tear my mother's dresses when locked in a dark closet), I now began to pick up paper clips when I saw them in the corridors. Self-consciously at first; later, with the conviction that it was practicing the principles of A.A. I even faced the memory of having torn my wife's dresses when she left me during my drunks. Those were the acts of a little boy, left in a closet of loneliness by his "mother." I began to understand that I was emotionally diseased—not morally bad.

Three years and nine months of working with the California Department of Corrections program passed, and I was paroled.

My word to you inside will be hard for you to take: quit planning for the outside in terms of a magic change in you at the gate. You change *now* or *never*. Nor is it important that you get out next year. The important deal is: prepare yourself now for then. The parole board has its eye on you. A ripe apple is plucked in season. The members have learned that green apples won't sell; that the green apples come back to them. I earnestly thank God as I understand Him that I did not get out until I was ready to cope with my problems as an emotionally maturing individual.

I felt no childish thrill when I walked through the gate. Just a sense of responsibility. I knew I was the same man who had been on the other side of the wall a few moments ago. Nothing had changed but my environment. I had the tools to dig into it. For the first time in my life I had no vague anxiety, no fear of life. I liked people. There was no desire to get even for what had been done to me; merely the sincere desire to live my gratitude for what had been done for me.

It is wonderful to be free from the prison of immature emotional patterns. All my life I'd been squeezed out of shape by that Chinese foot-binding process that is immaturity. Now I can walk among men who understand my slight limp.

Tomorrow—and all the tomorrows to come—are but extensions of *right here, right now*. That is the "out" for those inside; the "in" to the program for those outside. That is the real freedom for emotional growth that leads to maturity.

Anon., Santa Barbara, California

Every Tuesday and fourth Saturday

Normally, when I start talking about my life, I start at the beginning. If I was to do that, Grapevine would have to make it a special edition. So to sum things up I will simply say I was powerless, unmanageable, down and out, and a bum. I had tried to take my life three times, the last was four weeks before my incarceration. I was the loneliest person on earth.

At the age of twenty I was sent to Taycheedah Correctional Institution for five years. I knew I had a drinking problem, but an alcoholic—never. I joined the A.A. program here in T.C.I. because the staff told me I had to. I was in A.A. for a good impression on the parole board.

I attended A.A. in prison for a year and a half before I actually admitted to myself that I was an alcoholic. I believe that I'd still be kidding myself if it wasn't for an outside speaker sharing his experience. He talked about himself, but I saw me, within every word he spoke. Then I came to believe, admit, and accept that I, too, was an alcoholic. My only problem was that I only worked my program every Tuesday and fourth Saturday of the month.

Shortly afterward, I was transferred to a pre-release center for women. My big test, and freedom, all stood in this center. I made it through twenty-three months of prison sobriety, now can I make it another six months?

Two days after my two-year birthday I had a drink, right there in the center. I was still attending A.A. outside of the center, but lying to my sponsor, fellow members, and myself that I was still sober. I told myself that I would prove this world wrong and show them I knew how to drink socially.

Boy, was I wrong—two months later I found myself sitting in the county jail waiting to return to prison. I wasn't even free, and already I was on my way back. That was my bottom!

Since my return, my eyes have been opened to my real illness. I was not made to drink as a socializer.

I'm back in my A.A. program here in prison. And this time I live and work my program every day. I have both my sponsor and God to thank for helping me. Without them, I'd still be drunk, or I'd be dead.

I'm twenty-two years old now, still incarcerated, and will be [for another year]. With the grace of God by my side, I can make it—one day at a time.

A.C., Taycheedah, Wisc.

Prisoner A.A.

No man who has not served time in prison can understand or appreciate the problems that face inmates. A conducted tour of the penitentiary, talks with the men, and even letters to them cannot give one the insight necessary to be of much help. There is always a barrier between: one man has freedom, the other does not. Though friendship can develop, it is a friendship of strangers, and it takes something more than that to bind these two opposites together. This is where A.A. can fill the gap.

The A.A. program does not recognize walls. It is immune to the conditions which break down an individual relationship, the difference in social levels, of intellect, of experience. A.A. takes no heed of this. It has one primary law, help your fellow man and do it by example rather than by instruction. It is a strange organization in that it wants only failures for members. Nor does it advertise its virtues or actively seek converts. The man who needs help must want it before A.A. can be of any value. When this is asked, then this group of anonymous men, who have fought through the temptations of alcohol to respectability and compassion for others fighting the same battle, are ready to give aid. They show the way that they have taken to restoration of character and tell the beginner that it is up to him whether he wants to follow that course. If he does, it will call for personal honesty, a selfless devotion to helping others, and a belief in a power greater than himself. He is told that others stand beside him, ready to help, but that they cannot make him take the first step, he must do that himself.

A.A.'s greatest power is not in the program itself, but in the examples of the men who have followed it. They are individuals reborn, citizens of the highest order because their first precept is to help where help is wanted. Selfishness and its companions of bitterness and intolerance can hardly dwell where this principle burns with such a healing flame.

A.A. is especially needed in prison because an inmate is too prone to turn within, to brew a rancid cup of hate and distaste for all humanity. He needn't try to be responsible, needn't try to rebuild. The penitentiary is his mother, clothing, feeding and guarding him. He can become a baby and let moral and spiritual decay destroy whatever may have been good in him. And when he leaves prison, he will carry nothing but rot inside. It will fester and erupt, and the sickness of his disease will return him to the penitentiary where he will moulder and die.

Or he can choose A.A. He can make an effort to come back through an organization that places responsibility for success on him. He can fail and yet be welcomed back, can come to it with prejudice and personal gain as his reasons for attendance, yet not be turned away. However, he will discover that as long as such an attitude resides within him, he will continue to fail. Maybe he will accept the principles of selflessness that are the key to triumph. Or perhaps he'll sulk back to his cell as blind and doomed to habitual criminality as he was before. But even if he comes, he will find a new world opening. He will discover that he is not a forgotten being behind walls, but that there are men outside who wish to help him, if he will take the first step forward. A.A. is the bridge to that outside help, stronger than the help of one person alone.

An inmate will find through A.A. that a worthwhile life inside prison means a successful life outside, and that the fear of returning to a penitentiary need never be with him again. One way lies certain failure, the other way lies renewed opportunity to recover something valuable from all the years that he has wasted. Only a fool would refuse to try.

H. T. B., in "The Pioneer,"
Washington State Penitentiary

Bright promise

Three years ago an official prognosis for rehabilitation in my case would have read "hopeless." An alcoholic who could not hold a job, divorced, estranged from my parents, I came and went through prison gates like an official—except that I remained behind the walls a longer period of time. After my fourth conviction I was hopelessly confused and could see nothing in my future but an endless cycle of prison years.

Today I have regained my confidence, my integrity, my maturity. Tomorrow holds a bright promise for the first time in twenty-three years. After electro-shock treatment, aversion "cures," psychoanalysis, and delirium tremens had failed to straighten out my thinking, A.A. came to prison; and I came eagerly to A.A. It's wonderful! After forty-five years of trying to escape from life, I have just now begun to live!

In A.A. I have found friendship, sympathetic understanding, and experienced guidance along the road to sobriety. I have found myself; I have rediscovered my God.

The Twelve Steps have become to me not merely a means whereby I can control a twenty-three-year addiction to alcohol, but it is a philosophy of life that makes prison routine more bearable, and leads to new adventures in living. The Serenity Prayer is my bulwark against the many frustrations in prison life; and it is a sure cure for dry drunks.

Serenity to accept the things I cannot change . . . How one needs serenity in prison! Every minute, every hour, in the chaotic turmoil of argument and flaring anger that obtrudes in an eight-man cell; through the monotonous routine that nibbles at the edges of one's mind until the strong man breaks forth in violence, and the weaker man becomes a mental patient.

Courage to change the things I can . . . means that I can change my old pessimistic outlook and become constructive and positive in my thinking. I can mould the old personality over into one that will face up to the realities and responsibilities of life rather than one that seeks refuge in a bottle. To a small extent I find I can even change my environment so that my small portion of the cell becomes a private classroom for study, or a place of quiet meditation when prayer is needful—as it often is.

Another of my bulwarks against the confused thinking that brought me to prison is the Tenth Step: "Continued to take personal inventory." Each evening I review the happenings of the day. Whom have I hurt? Whom have I helped? Did I give my best to the job? What can I do tomorrow that will help me become more tolerant, more congenial?

The most difficult thing a man can do, I think, is to turn his eyes inward upon his real self. But I have learned through bitter experience that if I intend to grow into emotional stability and to enter into the maturity of adulthood, I *must* look upon my many shortcomings with an open, understanding mind, see them for what they are, and take steps to correct them.

And because A.A. is a spiritual program, I have gained a new conception of God.

Most prisoners scoff at religion. But A.A. is not a religion; it has no dogma, creed nor doctrine. It offers simple suggestions that can lead to a new way of life. It gives one back faith. Not faith in man-made creeds or obscure metaphysical tenets, but simple faith in God and the conviction that as individuals we are important and have a place and a value in this world.

Faith cured my inner conflict. Where once I warred with myself, I am now at peace. I accept my problems as necessary to my growth and take pleasure in solving them. I make friends and keep them. I have learned that before I criticize another I had better first examine my own faults. I have gained through A.A. a peace of mind and serenity of soul that I would not exchange for anything in the world—not even for freedom. For I am free now; prison walls cannot confine my thoughts nor undermine my confidence, that a useful, productive life awaits me when this sentence is completed.

I have learned that no man walks alone. Not when he has faith and trust in a power greater than himself; not when he no longer doubts, but *believes*.

Anon., U. S. Penitentiary,
Atlanta, Georgia

A reason for living

I belong to the Vision Group here in the Collins Bay institution. I don't wish to go into detail about why I'm serving a four-year sentence for manslaughter, but I would like to share some of the experiences that have happened to me since I've sobered up through the Fellowship of A.A.

When I woke up in jail, I knew immediately that I had a problem with booze. I guess you could say that I had hit my bottom. I joined A.A. while I was awaiting trial, and I also had the opportunity to attend a treatment center for alcoholism. While in A.A. on the street, I got active and associated with members all the time. I managed to stay sober, for some reason; I look back now and realize that it wasn't my doing, but that of a higher power of some sort. I had tried various ways to keep sober before, but they had all proved unsuccessful.

Now that I am in A.A., I am beginning to see things a lot different than I did when I was drinking. Now, I have a reason for living. The joint life isn't the easiest life to live, but I believe that each one of us has a purpose and that my Higher Power directed me here. I know that wherever I may be, there will always be A.A., and with that, I believe, I can survive anywhere.

When I came here, I immediately got involved with the program. This may sound unusual, but when I walked through the doors here to my first meeting, it felt like I had come home. I continued to attend meetings, and the group elected me secretary. I have heard people say that A.A. groups in prison are about the strongest groups going. I am not suggesting that A.A.s should go to prison! But if they were to attend a few meetings there and see the fellowship that the inmates have to offer, I'm sure that they would agree.

I am also editor-secretary of our A.A. newsletter, and I get to write to a lot of members out of the institution. I am very fortunate that I can devote the majority of my time to helping others with the same problem that I have. Sometimes, I wonder if this illness isn't a gift rather than a problem. I still have my bad days, but now I know what to do about them. When I received my one-year medallion, that was the most satisfying moment I have had since becoming a member.

Last year, we started a Seventh Tradition (group self-support) for the members inside the prison, and we hope to be giving a medallion to a few more members in the near future. I wish to say thanks to all the wonderful people that shook my hand when I needed it and gave me a cup of coffee. I know that without them I would be nowhere, with nothing.

R. D., Kingston, Ont.

Balancing the books

My first experience of freedom came while I was locked up in the state penitentiary. I had been carefully guided through the first seven Steps and had begun to awaken spiritually. I trusted the A.A. process and was beginning to trust God.

But my sponsors and I were faced with a logistical problem. No matter how willing we were to make direct amends, the state would not let us out to do so. One of my sponsors had committed murder, and for him to directly contact the victim's family would cause much undue harm.

As we discussed these issues, it became clear that the key to the Eighth Step was willingness; if this God were truly loving and merciful as it appeared, we would not be kept in bondage simply because we could not reach those to whom we owed restitution. Freedom would come, it seemed, when I stood entirely ready to make amends wherever possible.

My sponsor gave me an exercise to do. I was to make a list of all the people I had harmed. This list would start with the names from my inventory. It was suggested that there were many others I had harmed that also must go on the list, even though there was no resentment or fear connected with them. I was to be as clear as possible as to the harm I had done. *But*—my sponsor pointed out—even though I knew what I had done to each person, I was so insensitive that I probably did not know the consequences of my actions. He gave me the key to freedom; I was to close my eyes and picture each person separately in front of me. I was to look each straight in the eye and see if I could feel a willingness to say: "I have been wrong and have caused you harm. Will you please tell me what I must do so that we can get the books to balance?" As I sat in the cell that night going over my list, I had the experience I had been looking for all my life: I was lifted and set free.

In my blindness I had always believed that a spiritual awakening was the end of the road. Now, having had one, I knew it was but the beginning. Finally, at thirty-four years of age, I could truly begin to live.

Don P., Aurora, Colo.

24

It could happen to you

Can you remember those times when you awoke and were unable to get out of bed unless you knew where there was a drink hidden around the house? The day that I went on the drunk that landed me behind the walls for fifteen years, was no different from several hundred others.

When I started out that morning, it was just another day. I didn't have any idea that something would happen that, in my warped way of thinking, would cause me to go berserk, cause me to forget myself to the extent that I would want to do harm to other people.

Arriving at prison, I was entering a way of life that seemed to be the end of everything for me. Friends, family, acquaintances all gone, not wanting to have anything to do with me. Why? Who was to blame? How did I ever let myself get into the mess into which I had fallen? Sick in mind, body, and soul, and to top all of it I was slowly going blind.

Where was old faithful? John Barleycorn, the friend that had sustained you for so many years . . . how could he desert you at such a time?

Then the guard comes around and tells you to come on out, let's go see the man. Shaking and sick, you make your way outside to give someone information about yourself. The questions are those you cannot answer or do not care even to try. They hammer at you for the details of your crime, when you may not be sure that you committed any at all.

What can I do? What will I do?

These questions sound simple—to those who have never become slaves to alcohol. Ask the alcoholic the same questions and see what kind of an answer you receive. I was unable even to try to answer them. Yet the man who was interrogating me expected an answer. He was not interested in *why* I was here or the crime that I had committed. It was his job to get the information that was needed to fill out the papers to start my prison record.

To me it was the end.

What could I do for myself? That question had to be answered, and fast. In my early childhood, my parents sent me to church several times a week, but in my roving over the country I had neglected to keep up the training that they had tried so hard to instill into me. And I knew that the view I now held of Christianity would never pull me out of the rut I was in. In jail, awaiting the chain to drag me here, I met a fellow who had belonged to an outfit called A.A. In talking to him I could see that in many respects our lives had run a parallel course. He advised me to investigate the A.A. group at the penitentiary.

Thank God, I *did* investigate.

I asked for and was given permission to attend meetings in the Pioneer Group. I was amazed at the ex-winos I saw there telling about the new way of life. Could I, Barney, admit that I was unable to handle my drinking? Heck, no. Who ever dreamed up such a program with so much hooey in it? Me, I could manage my life without joining a bunch of nuts.

But the bug must have taken a liking to me, for the next meeting night I was there again, trying to sneer at everything that was said. No one said anything that made sense to me, or at least I wanted it to be that way. Still, I would be waiting for the next meeting. Finally after many months and many talks it began to sink into my thick skull that there was something here that I was overlooking. What? I didn't know. But I intended to find out.

I started to take inventory.

I found that I was guilty of everything implied in living the reverse of A.A.'s Twelve Steps, plus the fact I had forsaken God as I understood Him. What to do about it? First, get right with God as I understood Him. Second, go to work on the Twelve Steps and not just say I will take it easy until I find my way, but get out and work each Step as if it meant my life—which it did. It is surprising what we can find out about the program, and God as we understand Him, if we just try. It doesn't take half as much effort as it did to stay drunk.

You ask, "Is this program *easy* in prison?" No! No! No! There is a sign at most railroad crossings, STOP-LOOK-LISTEN. Change that to read, STOP-LOOK-and THINK.

Is it easy to admit that we are unable to manage our life? No. Admit we are not sane? No. Is it easy to turn our will and our life over to the care of God as we understand Him, after the years we have spent drinking? No. Easy to make a searching and fearless moral inventory? No. Easy to admit to God and ourselves and another human being our mistakes? I should say not. Are we ready to have God remove these shortcomings? No. Ready to ask Him to remove our defects? No. Ready to make a list of those that we have harmed in order to make amends? No. Are we ready to continue to take personal inventory and admit when we are wrong? Who ever heard of such foolishness? Are we willing to seek through prayer and meditation to draw nearer to God? No. We do not have time to carry this message to other alcoholics. Let them shift for themselves.

Can this program *become* easy in prison? Yes. If a person is sincere; if he really wants to do something about the mess he has made of his life—the way it is worked in prison is not much different than on the outside. Oh yes, I can hear many say there are not as many temptations in prison as there are outside on the street. You can forget that too. There are just as many, if not more ways, to foul up the program in here as there are out there.

When you take the Twelve Steps and look them over, there are, to my way of counting them, eleven that deal with the spiritual side. Am I right? What does the word *spiritual* mean? To me it means that I have become convinced that there is a power that is greater than I; that to be able to go to that power for help, I must forget about trying to take advantage of some "fish" that has just arrived . . . forget about trying to get some pills to go on a jag . . . lying to others, going out of my way to keep from doing someone a favor, or expecting a material gain from all favors that I do. Is that working the program? Is that the way it is worked outside? I can only answer for the inside, and I say No! If we are sincere about the Twelve Steps, we can do it. If we are not, then why fool with it at all?

We are only looking for one thing from the A.A. program. Sobriety, right? If we are looking for something else, my personal opinion is we are just wasting time. For we will never *stay* sober if we are looking only for ways to get out, or for a shorter sentence. Forget about A.A.

I know you can make A.A. work in prison, but you have to learn tolerance and become willing to let the Higher Power help you every day, in everything. Learn to be honest with yourself, God, and others. Each day try to change your many faults, but don't get the idea you are perfect. Be sure to make all meetings. Sure, I know that after three, five, ten years we get tired of seeing the same old faces, but just remember, the ones that are still out there from our group are the ones who practiced their tolerance.

What happened to the blindness that I mentioned in the beginning? Yes, I went blind. But, through faith in the power that I admitted was higher than I (yes, thanks to Him,) after an operation I recovered fair sight in one eye. Someday soon I hope to have the other one back too. Would this have come true outside? I don't know. Truthfully, I doubt it. Knowing myself and the way I loved the pain-easer, alcohol, I am sure death would have been the outcome long before this.

Barney B., Pioneer Group,
Washington State Penitentiary

When you hit the streets—call A.A.

In April 1973, in a courtroom I had been attending faith-fully (thirteen appearances), I was sentenced to an insti-tution for five years to life. Well, let me tell you, I'd been locked up a few times before, but this time it was differ-ent. Facing five to life was a big one!

The judge's last words were: "I am going to sentence you to the institution for the criminally insane for an indefinite period of time. And by the way, there is a good A.A. program there."

I must admit I forgot those words until about a week later, when I heard one of the other inmates ask the guards to unlock the ward so he could go to the A.A. meeting. At that moment, things started to connect. The man in the black robe flashed in front of me. Call it what you want, but today I call it a spiritual experience.

I liked my first meeting. I saw some outsiders, and the women were not bad-looking. The coffee was good, and they even raffled off cigarettes and cigars. What more could I ask for than having Friday and Saturday nights out?

I figured that if I was going to stay in there for a while, I might as well make it as comfortable as possible. After several meetings, I must have started listening a little bit, because I wanted what some of those people had—freedom, peace, property, money, prestige, women! I kept going, started to read the Big Book, and got a little involved with the program. I started to listen and to work some of the principles into my incarcerated life. It paid off. After two years, I was released on five-year probation.

When I hit the streets, that's when it all came down. I was an ex-con, full of fright, elation, apprehension, happiness, confusion. I had been told again and again that when I hit the streets, I should contact A.A., no matter what. But I was so wrapped up in myself and the goings-on around me that I had no time even to think of A.A. I had more important things to do—renew my driver's license, buy new clothes, sex. I alternated between elated feelings of finally being free and fear of facing the world again. I felt as if I had "ex-con" tattooed all over me, and every time I saw a cop, I had paranoia.

I'd sit at home on the sofa, watching TV, and feel I should get going, boogie, get it on. Then I would pop a few candy bars and sodas down my throat, remembering that someone had told me sugar would keep me cool and I wouldn't want to drink. Was I lonely! Maybe just one soft drink at one of the bars I pass? But will they ask me who I am? Will they *know* who I am? So I wouldn't go out. I'd continue to watch TV, then go to bed.

After about three days of this, I went to my first "outside" A.A. meeting, filled with fear, ashamed, and knowing they would not like me. I wondered what they would think of me, an ex-con. Should I tell them I'm a newcomer? A visitor? Somehow, with all my confusion, I managed to drive to the meeting. Full of anxiety, head hung, I walked into that room.

"Welcome." I was welcomed, and that sure felt good. I got some coffee, and when it was my turn, I said, "My name is E——, and I am a grateful alcoholic." I can remember some of the people telling me everything was all right, no matter what—and please come back.

Now that I'm out—what now? I attend A.A. meetings all over the county and state. I love it! I get involved in almost all phases of this Fellowship. In the nearly five years since I've been out, I have found God's grace in the Fellowship, and hundreds of beautiful friends.

The only change I would make in the last five years would be to have contacted A.A. earlier. But my Higher Power carried me over some dangerous ground. I got past it, and learned enough to set that lesson down on paper and let somebody else know that it is going to be okay.

Today, I can honestly say that I am grateful for the prison system, and to the people working in it. Without them, I would not have A.A. and would not be able to share my experience with you.

E. M., Santa Barbara, Calif.

The perfect welcome

Not many alcoholics in A.A. had to pay the price for membership that I did: imprisonment. As a result of my Battle of the Bottle, I landed eventually in South Walpole, where the Massachusetts Correctional Institution is located—better known as State Prison.

It was in that institution that I came in contact with A.A. I shall be forever grateful to the Norwood A.A. Group, which visits South Walpole A.A. Group Number Thirteen each Wednesday, and to A.A. members of greater Boston who came to the prison weekly. It was there, still in prison, that I learned I did not have to drink, and that through the Twelve Suggested Steps of A.A. my life could become rehabilitated.

When I left prison on parole, I faced life with a new and brighter outlook as far as the booze problem was concerned. But almost at once another problem developed—that of being branded an ex-con. The general public is just not educated to the fact that a criminal is a sick person morally. People just do not look down the long road of circumstances—in my case booze—which leads to imprisonment. But in A.A. groups here in New Hampshire, I was accepted. It added much to my humility to be asked to speak at meetings, as well as to chair meetings.

After telling my story many times in A.A. meetings, and telling it honestly, I have never once had a member of A.A. demonstrate prejudice against me. The hearty handshake at the end of a meeting gives me the sense of belonging. These are my people; these are my friends (and real friends). "Ex-con" is never thrown in my face. I am just another alcoholic, trying by God's grace to live the A.A. program twenty-four hours at a time.

Not to take the other guy's or gal's inventory, but . . . I have seen men take advantage of A.A. in prison. Standing before the State Parole Board, it makes a good impression to belong to A.A. But A.A., as I found it to be, is for one thing, one purpose only—to keep an alcoholic such as myself sober. An inmate in prison cannot bluff when it comes to A.A. He is only kidding himself. If his prime objective is to get out of prison, then as sure as he is an alcoholic he will get drunk and will return again.

I have had friends in A.A. who have given me a hand when the going got tough. But here the fine line between charity and A.A.'s Twelfth Step must be drawn. A.A., as such, is not a charitable organization. It is not in the small loan business, though countless unknown charitable acts may be credited to individual A.A. members. But here, too, the ex-convict must realize that members of A.A. are not idiots. They realize when they are being taken. And what is more important, A.A. members almost at once detect when a person is not sincere.

It is difficult for an alcoholic ex-convict to find and hold a job, unless he is absolutely honest. Certainly, his employer *must* know his background. As the general public is educated to the effectiveness of the A.A. program, understanding men in the business world will tend more and more to accept members of A.A. as employees, even those with past criminal records. In fact, there is reason to hope that employers might favor alcoholics who have recovered in A.A. over those who refuse to do anything about their drinking problem, in many instances.

But to return to my own story: it is in an A.A. meeting that I feel at home. I am relaxed there, for I know that never will a finger be pointed at me. We learn to live in A.A. by our motto: "But for the Grace of God"; and most humbly I thank God for the true friends He has given me, an ex-con, in Alcoholics Anonymous.

R.S., Laconia Group, N.H.

Freedom began in prison

The Starlight Bowl is a lovely outdoor concert auditorium, set deep between canyon walls, high above "beautiful downtown Burbank" in California. This summer night held particular significance for me. My ten-year-old daughter Cindy was with me, her silky golden hair spread over my knees as she rested her head on my lap. We were listening to the delightful strains of "Tales From the Vienna Woods," at a concert by the Burbank Symphony Orchestra.

It hadn't always been this way. . . .

Several years before this memorable night, I was released from a state prison, a stranger to my daughter and very apprehensive about how I'd behave in free society. I'd never been able to cope with freedom before.

Six years before my release, I stood at the bar in a local tavern with a pistol in my hand. I was a practicing alcoholic and desperately needed money to continue my latest drunk. Being too proud to beg, having run out of friends and family, and feeling the fantastic courage granted by much red wine, I was attempting robbery. Fortunately for the bar owner (and, as it turned out, for me), I was captured in the midst of my bumbling crime. The police treated me fairly, even kindly. The court procedures passed swiftly, and within three months I was on the way to a state prison. I was to remain there three years.

This three-year period became the greatest, most productive time I'd spent in all my thirty years up to that point. During my confinement, I again became active in my church, relearning many basic precepts of good living. I used the library facilities intensely, reading widely on philosophy and alcoholism. Most important of all, I became an involved, active participant in A.A.

Delving deeply into the Twelve Steps under the adept guidance of the free A.A. members who came in twice a week, I was soon writing my Fourth Step inventory. Having completed this written confession to myself, I made arrangements with the prison staff to have an outside A.A. member come in to hear my Fifth Step. We were provided with a private office and coffee, and spent three hours reviewing the sordid details of my past. It

was the first such occurrence in that particular institution, and it worked out so well that many men since then have been able to complete their Fourth and Fifth Steps while still incarcerated.

This inventory-taking was the turning point of my life. An almost immediate freedom from all guilt and remorse came upon me. I was literally free from my past. It was during this time that I learned what true freedom was. It had nothing to do with walls and guards—it had to do with a feeling inside. Freedom is a state of mind.

Today, I cherish my physical and emotional freedom with all my heart and soul. In order of precedence, it stands second only to sobriety. What an education A.A. has given to me! Everything I am or have belongs to A.A. in reality. More than tangible benefits, A.A. has given me a way to go, a way to live and live happily and abundantly.

Many blessings have been showered upon me during my five years and nine months of sobriety—great spiritual gifts, as well as the more ordinary supplies of money and goods. These great gifts come one after the other in spite of my own foolishness and fumbling, as I very slowly grope my way towards the light of reason and love. The good things increase in direct proportion to my willingness to become more teachable and humble in my daily affairs.

And so it is that a chronic daily drunk, discarded by free society, hating and rejecting the very society that spawned him, can come to enjoy what many "free" people may take for granted: a simple concert, a wonderful summer night filled with beautiful music, and a sweet little child who loves and trusts her daddy.

R. R., Universal City, Calif.

A thing called hope

I am an incarcerated alcoholic. I am only thirty-one years of age, but have been drinking for nineteen of them. I also began to use drugs shortly after my first drink; however, my preference was always alcohol. Even when I was using another drug, there was always alcohol involved. This part of my story is no different from hundreds of others that I'm sure you have heard. I went through many short-lived jobs, and was kicked out of the worst of flophouses because of my drinking behavior. At one point I chose not to continue to pay the rent on my furnished room (paid by welfare check) because I could keep that much more money to drink with. This was insanity, as it was the dead of winter, and not having friends or any relatives, I made my home(s) between the benches at the Astor Place and Broad Street subway stations in New York City. Whenever a cop would wake me at one and send me on my way, I would head to my other home.

For approximately the last ten years of my drinking, everyone around me saw my trouble—the social workers at welfare, the judges (I've been arrested seventy-two times), the probation officers. They referred me to various treatment programs, which in turn all used A.A. as a supportive tool in their treatment. However, "I was not an alcoholic" and resented the very fact that they could even think I was. Needless to say, without that first step I never sobered up. I bring this up so that you realize that I had been led to the water, but would not drink of it.

Each time I wound up in jail, it was usually for about ninety days. I would get out and head straight to the liquor store—my freedom was always short-lived. I cannot remember ever getting out and not thinking that I would come back again. It was only a question of how long this time.

In the last five years I had come to believe that my life was cursed. I tried to kill myself six times (I couldn't even do that right).

When I got to this prison, I began going to the A.A. meetings so that I could impress the parole board and win an early release. Well, that didn't work. When I made my appearance before them they "hit" me. They extended my sentence; the state was going to get every day from me that they could legally claim under this sentence.

Then something strange happened; now that A.A. had no chance of winning me an early release date, I kept on attending. Somewhere, somehow, something was said in one of those meetings that gave me something I had never had before. Today I can name that something; it is called *hope*! I heard people come in from outside and speak; people who had been as bad off as I was, and others who had not gotten that bad yet. Some had even been in prison before, but they all spoke of being happy today. I could tell that they weren't lying because you could see the happiness all over their faces. I decided that I wanted what they had, and became more involved. I began to read the Big Book, the Twelve and Twelve, *As Bill Sees It,* and *Alcoholics Anonymous Comes of Age.* And today I anxiously await each month's Grapevine—I have even managed to get about two hundred back issues that have become my favorite reading. Quite often when I am reading them my eyes fill up with tears, for I feel that newfound hope deep inside. Today, I have a responsible job here in the prison, as a peer counselor in the pre-release center. I have gotten an outside sponsor who comes in once a week to visit me, and he has been helping me to work the Steps. Through putting those Steps into my life, I have become an honest person whom people are not afraid to trust or depend on. I have even been elected chairman of our small meeting in here.

As of this writing, I have sixty-six days left until my sentence is complete and I will be released. Today, I do not even think how long it will be before I come back next time. Never before have I gotten out without that thought.

If the program can give me a sense of hope, an actual sense of serenity, even in a place like this, then I want more of it when I get out. I have already chosen my first A.A. meeting not too far from this prison. I know that now I must do as so many others before me have so unselfishly done, and give away what was given so freely to me.

I would like to extend my heartfelt thanks to all those wonderful A.A.s who took the time out to come into this prison, which houses those declared unfit to be a part of society by the courts, so that we could receive the message that they had to share with us.

W.H., Bedford Hills, N.Y.

I found freedom in prison

What my unreal world most needed was a bar mirror that gave back true images of the Alice's and Alec's in Blunderland.

Many years ago, I sat at a bar drinking expensive Scotch and watching a Man-Who-Never-Was in the bottle-lined looking glass. It was a bad case of a mutual admiration in full bloom for, Narcissus-like, I was in love with my own reflection. I saw a super-brilliant lawyer, a fast-buck buccaneer above the law and the original big shot destined to be heard around the world.

The blackout. . . .

I sat in a skidrow room, wages for washing dishes a mark of a retrieved affluence after years of nomadic alcoholism. I sat and looked down at three winos huddled against the side of a dingy building in the rain, counting pennies. Four bottles of muscatel were on my table and I felt only contempt for the bums shivering in the rain. I was still superior . . . but I was no longer a lawyer. The taste of peat smoke had long been replaced by synthetic grape on my tongue.

Big shot? A smart aleck in Blunderland. . . .

Several days later I walked into a drugstore with a toy pistol (minus caps) in my hand and told a diminutive druggist I was taking over. He took me over without so much as a faint *pop* from my toy pistol. So much for the big shot that was to be heard around the world.

I was sentenced to prison as a recidivist to serve an indeterminate term under the California Department of Corrections. The classic Greek theme faded: It was Narcissus who died; only Echo remained.

There is no hell like the searing realization that one has come to the end of one's resources. I had no friends, no money. I had only the past—Echo. Somewhere in the future I would have to face a parole board on a record rubber-stamped "Nomadic Alcoholic." That is no mark of distinction to influence people and win freedom. I was fifty-three years of age, disbarred and without any tools to rebuild a new life. The present was black, utterly without hope.

One still, black night—when Echo whistled like a cold wind around dead Narcissus—I turned to God as I understand Him. I didn't ask Him for freedom in return for great deeds after my release. That lie was old in His ears. I just said: "Please, God, call me back to life from this death." A little later, I began asking him to let me become a writer. I'd never been a fiction writer but God and writing were all that were left to me.

I began attending Alcoholics Anonymous in prison. It is one of the therapeutic programs sponsored by the Care & Treatment Division of the California Department of Corrections. At first it seemed so futile. . . . I couldn't get a drink if I had wanted one.

A year passed. I began to learn that drinking is a symptom of a personality sickness—an obsession of the mind, an allergy of the body. I discovered that I could get on emotional jags in prison. In fact, that I couldn't help getting on those jags. That's when I really got scared. I was powerless over my emotional pattern—and that was the pattern which, on the outside, drove me into barrooms. My reactions to frustrations flooded me with resentments and I lived a bitter and sordid life in a cell. Gradually I came to realize that this pattern, so apparent to me on the inside, was no different from what it had been on the outside. I was doomed to die an alcoholic in prison or out. Then, somewhere along the line, I stepped from the inside of the prison to the inside of me. What I was inside of me was what I was outside of me in my actions. I knew then that every alcoholic in this world, wherever he might be, was a prisoner. . . .

It was too big a problem to face alone. That is how I came to admit that I am an alcoholic and how I came to believe that a power greater than myself, if sought, can and will restore me to sanity.

I sought that power in every channel available to me: in Alcoholics Anonymous, in my church, in group counseling and in individual counseling. Some of this good coming in had to flow out. I served as secretary of our prison A.A. group, on the steering committee, and as a speaker. Don't ask me how this program works, but the bitterness and the sordidness gradually faded out of the picture.

This power began to fill in the shriveled potential of the guy whose selfishness had all but cost him his soul.

This is the way it works. One begins to see one's faults in the faults of others and one grows less critical of one's fellow man. Empathy is born. The nerve-racking confinement has no sting for the man who *lives* the program. God grants one the serenity to accept the things one cannot change, the courage to change the things one can, and experience teaches one the wisdom to know the difference. Life in prison became a high adventure, zestful, full of promise, replete with day-by-day progress toward perfection. *I found freedom in prison.*

Meantime, I was writing fiction. The steel bands that had restricted writing to wishful thinking snapped. I think empathy dissolved them. For I was able to see the other fellow's problems, his viewpoint. My characters came alive. In a short fourteen months I have sold nineteen short stories, paid an income tax in prison, and have a novel and twelve stories in the mill. All in addition to an eight-hour-a-day clerical job. More important still, I'm revising the story of my life so that the "you's" and "they's" play as prominent a part as the "I's" in this new script. It's a balanced story. . . .

Thank you, God, for A.A. and dreams come true.

T. W., San Luis Obispo, Calif.

With the aid of A.A., my life took another path

I am definitely an alcoholic. I drank for fifteen years before I got sober. I started at the age of fourteen, and from the very start, every time I drank, I would drink to get drunk, and every time I got drunk, I got into trouble with the law.

I have spent a lot of time dealing with staying sober while in prison. I have been sober for the past six years, all the while being incarcerated. It wasn't easy! In fact, there were times when I came within a hair of getting drunk. I know today that if I had taken a drink on those occasions, my life would surely have taken another course while in prison, and a course requiring more dues to be paid than I could afford.

My last drunk brought me to my knees in total surrender to the fact that I was powerless over alcohol and in admission to myself that I had a disease called alcoholism. Even though I got sober physically, I was still drunk emotionally and mentally, which continued to affect the way I thought and lived. In the past, these feelings would have forced me to escape to the security of my bottle. But in prison, I sought the solace of A.A., upon the urgent suggestion of my wife and my A.A. sponsor.

In the beginning, I could never understand the need for A.A. in jail, when access to alcohol was limited and all my thoughts were concerned with my family, those I had hurt, and the legal proceedings that faced me. I knew that my being an alcoholic was the primary factor in my arrest, but I couldn't understand the constant need for getting to A.A. meetings. However, I kept going —in body, but not in mind. I knew I had to be there, for I knew I was an alcoholic. I was searching for a way to rid myself of all the fears I carried, and to be able to live life as normally as did those around me who were sober.

With many meetings, and reading about Alcoholics Anonymous in my cell, I came to learn that the A.A. program is far more than abstinence from alcohol. It is an all-new way of life for the alcoholic who is willing to get sober. I learned that A.A. does not preach, but rather suggests. I further learned that A.A. (in prison or out) is for those who are really serious about wanting to be sober, and has but one primary purpose: sobriety.

As my body became free of alcohol, my thinking gradually started to sober up. The thought of drinking kept coming up at times when the crew I associated with indulged in it. When this happened, I had a decision to make, and only I could make it. I openly told those around me that I was an alcoholic, and if they respected me, they would count me out.

In the beginning, I would hear such things as "You can't be serious about all those things they say in A.A.," or "A couple of cups won't hurt you." It was times like this that made me immediately think back to my last arrest, when I was on my hands and knees, suffering from the results of alcohol in my life and in the lives of those I loved. Such thoughts of reality gave me the courage to keep saying no, and as time progressed, all those around me came to respect my wish not to indulge. Many times, it was still a struggle to say no, especially when I was feeling depressed, angered, or resentful. At these times, I would also recall a slogan my sponsor always used to repeat to me: "simple—not easy!"

My jailhouse sobriety grew from days to weeks, and from months to years. With this new personal growth and the aid of A.A., the direction and interests in my life took another path, a path that was constructive and meaningful and gave sense to my existence. I found talents within me that I never knew I had, and found myself helping other people—something I had never done before. My involvement in A.A. grew with every new day of sobriety, and out of it grew the desire to participate, putting my sobriety above everything else. I know that without my sobriety, I could never have coped or dealt successfully with the past five and a half years, nor could I have accomplished all that I have in personal growth. Most important, I could never have done it alone, without the help of A.A. and all those connected with the Fellowship.

Today, I am sober, but I know that I am only one drink away from a drunk. Today, I can deal with the problems that confront me, and even though they become quite difficult at times, I know that I have the strength to accept and handle them today. My worst sober day is a million times better than any of my best past drinking days.

To me, sobriety in jail is no different from sobriety outside, in that it stems from following the Twelve Steps and Twelve Traditions of A.A., one day at a time. I am sober only today, and I am responsible only for today. Should something go wrong with the way I do things, then it is my warning that I am not following the suggested Steps of A.A. When this happens, I usually speak with a "winner" in the program, or with one of the alcoholism counselors. I also get into reading my literature, which I keep plenty of in my cell, and somewhere among the pages, I will find the remedy to my feelings and mood at the time. When I run into a rut or a problem, it is usually because I am not being honest with myself, and it's time for me to show real humility and admit my character defects.

My life today is manageable, and I am thankful to God for all that I have, and for all that I don't have. I know that if I don't drink today, I won't lose what I have gained, nor have to fear things will happen that I have no control over. I am grateful today for the awareness and knowledge I have of my disease, which I know now must be treated daily. I know that I must keep my life just as simple as Bill W. and Dr. Bob did while together they structured the Fellowship of Alcoholics Anonymous. It is a simple program, and a way of life that makes things get better beyond one's wildest imagination!

J. M., Woodbourne, N.Y.

Sobriety is an inside job

Being incarcerated for the past eighteen months in the Texas Department of Corrections has given me the sober opportunity to realize, examine, and begin to deal with some of my many character defects. I am an alcoholic. With the help of the A.A. program and a renewed faith in my Higher Power, I have experienced some amazing results and changes in my life. This required several action steps on my part. Fear had previously kept me from this.

For the biggest part of the last twenty-eight years, I drank excessive·y almost daily. It appeared to be a natural way of life. My first arrest for any reason was for

DWI on my forty-third birthday. At that time, this was simply a stroke of bad luck. Only two months later, it was followed by involuntary manslaughter and failure to stop and render aid. Then came a subsequent DWI, and here I am.

There were a few short dry periods during the two years before coming to prison. These were directly related to my attendance at A.A. meetings. Today, I have no resentments against anyone and no one to blame. I put me where I am today.

Shortly after coming to this unit, I was put to a real test for an alcoholic. Somehow, I managed to refuse that first drink of "chalk" offered to me—but it did smell good. Remembering the advice of an old friend in A.A., I conned my way past an officer and made my first meeting here without a pass. When asked, I found myself ready to speak at the first prison meeting to a group of men whom I had never met before. This helped to open the communications lines. Another thing I realized was that from positive action, some good results would occur. The fear that creates so many undesirable character defects had to be overcome, and it was up to me and only me to do this.

Being shy, because of fear, has been one of my worst defects of character. Mail call in the joint is the highlight of the day for most men in here. The desire to write to an A.A. member, whom I could communicate with effectively, was there, but so were the feelings of shame about myself. It was at this first meeting in prison that I picked up the A.A. pamphlet "It Sure Beats Sitting in a Cell." At that time, writing to an A.A. in my home area was impossible—they knew me. Following a suggestion in that pamphlet, I wrote to G.S.O. (the A.A. General

Service Office) for assistance in finding someone to correspond with.

This little action step resulted in a new method of communications for me, not only in A.A., but in several other areas also. Have you ever had a self-appointed (I appointed him) sponsor via mail? For more than a year, I have had regular correspondence with an A.A. in New Jersey. This is a man I have no photo of and have never talked to or seen, but I do know him. The letters are another A.A. meeting, and the meetings in prison are limited. For me, they are a very special kind of meeting, one that can be filed away for future reading and reminder, a cassette on paper. The help received in the form of suggestions based on A.A. experience, answers to various questions, some A.A. literature, encouragement and thanks, and just plain honest fellowship has had a dramatic effect on my life. This has happened in ways too numerous to list, but I will be forever grateful to my Higher Power and A.A. as a whole.

Writing is a very effective way to vent and/or express my thoughts, ideas, joys, and frustrations stemming from the negative atmosphere most inmates live in. Some of the old fear remains, but I'm working on that. Today, I have enough faith to attempt writing—so if you haven't tried it, don't knock it!

Among my many character defects, the refusal to ask for help probably ranked number two (fear being the worst). The self-inflated ego, coupled with fear, gave me a good false reason to get drunk many times. Shortly after coming to prison, I learned that there were some things I would have to ask for, without drinking booze, in order to make life here reasonably comfortable. The big ego had made me want to be independent in all matters. Ego deflation proved to be a strenuous task. Humility meant shame and degradation. With the help of A.A. and a lot of meditation, I began to realize how mentally deranged I had become. That was tough to swallow, but thanks to this program, I accepted it. Experiencing humility today is a cherished gift and a far cry from my original idea.

After several months in prison, my attitude toward people, places, things, and ideas was still very poor a lot of times. I hid this as best I could. The A.A. program was getting into a lot of areas of my life—what a revelation! Now another action step was required, because I had become more conscious of yet another character defect after these few months of youthful sobriety.

Our prison group is fortunate to have a few regular "free world" guest speakers. One of these men made a statement that really stuck with me. He said, "A.A. is more than just two letters designating Alcoholics Anonymous. It stands for Absolute Abstinence and Attitude Adjustment. The alcoholic must undergo an attitude adjustment." This made one hell of an impression on my mind. The lost art of listening and hearing was being returned, and I could comprehend things again. With effort on my part, I have managed to experience a lot of change in attitude, and all for the better. Once again, I have my Higher Power and A.A. to be grateful to.

Prison life is not a piece of cake. It would be easy to dwell on the negative aspects in a very negative atmosphere. Today, I have a choice, or should I say many choices. No longer is this a life of fear, self-pity, despair, loneliness, and hate. Today can be bad or beautiful; it is my choice. School or work, study or sleep, speak or remain silent—these are just a few of the choices I have today. Alcohol had taken away the freedom of choice and much more a long time before I came to prison. The realization of my imprisonment by alcohol was snuffed out by the substance itself.

I have not become institutionalized, and I am looking forward to my release. I was insane and fully admitted that in Step Two. This may come as a shock to some, but I fully believe that this trip to prison is a blessing for me. Hitting bottom is hard, but I have the sober opportunity to move ahead in the right direction; it could have been much worse. I will be forever grateful to God, the A.A. program, and the people in it for what has been so freely and generously given to me. Thanks!

L. P., Huntsville, Tex.

The parole violator

Just a matter of three months ago, "Yours Truly" went out into society ("free world" as they call it here) to live that long dreamed of life—that of a free man, a useful citizen in society again. With me, I took my eight years plus of A.A.; its teachings and philosophy, the experience of hearing of other's failures and successes, and a firm resolution that *I* was not going to be one of the failures. Not me.

Yet, here I am, back inside these grey walls, practically in the same cell, and on the same job that I began my prison term on nine years ago. What happened? I know, but it's hard to admit. I simply allowed myself to become too complacent and too self-satisfied with my A.A. The first few weeks I was out in the "world" again, I couldn't attend enough meetings to suit me. Night after night found me driving here and there over the Denver area. Then, I found myself missing these meetings and telling myself that I just couldn't be expected to attend so many. From five meetings a week I slipped to maybe one or two at the most; I began to find excuses as to why I couldn't attend. "Too tired tonight" or "Something has come up" or "I have a busy day tomorrow and I have to get to bed early," and so on.

A lot of people were telling me what a wonderful job I was doing in A.A. and bragged on my progress and it went to my ego-seeking head. Sure, I had started from scratch and in two months owned my car, a new truck and, of all things, a small bank account. But all that I gained and was so proud of was, in a way, the beginning of my return trip to prison as a violator and possibly more charges later on that will gain me a "new number" and more time here. Being so damn cocksure of myself and the progress that I was making, I began to make A.A. a secondary thing in my new life on the streets. No, my trouble wasn't the "gay night life" or the "pretty girls" who seem to hang around all the bars waiting for "Hoosiers" like me to show up, for I didn't touch an alcoholic drink until that fatal night when the lid flipped. I forgot that I was on parole.

Things began to crowd me, things that I had piled up on myself, the many responsibilities that I accepted and wasn't ready for yet, the many favors that others wanted done and that required my A.A. meeting time. So, fool that I am and always will be, I did neglect A.A. and the meetings. The term of "chicken" that people hung on me when I would refuse a drink, became just a little harder to take and finally I, in a weak moment, said "The hell with it," and so here I sit, back in this damn cell, wondering what really happened. My first and only drunk in nine years, the one that put me here, was a dandy, as the boys and girls around the bars say.

The rest is a matter of record now. I am back in prison, I have a lot of checks to make good, a lot of faith to restore in those who had trust in me, and I must begin again. All those friends whom I had made in the many bars and nightclubs that I had visited and drank in— they are gone now. The "good times" are a memory, all that is left are a lot of broken hearts and more time to serve. The hardest part is before me now, that of beginning again.

The Fourth Step is becoming more and more a big factor in my A.A. program and I must never forget that all important First Step again! Admission and personal inventory—those are the key words to working this program and when any alcoholic loses sight of this fact, then he may as well quit trying to work the program for he is defeating his own purpose—that of overcoming alcoholism—fooling himself, no one else. The sincere A.A. member who is working and living the A.A. program, can spot a phony a mile away, (wonder how many spotted me?) and yet it is not his place to tell him or work his program for him. A.A. is there for those who sincerely want it and seek it out.

This was my folly: I ceased to seek it out and thought that A.A. owed *me* something! Now, I am trying once again. I pray God that *this* time it will work, or rather, that *I* will work. There is so much in the Big Book that I missed before because I was too busy being a "wheel" and fooling myself. How long I will be here this time depends on those who direct our future, but you can bet on this: I will work it and live it, regardless of the wise-cracks and smart remarks that are passed my way because I am back here and back into the A.A. program; I am the one who has to live my life, they don't and, as it has been stated so many times in the meetings lately, I must grow up!

I must begin again, and with A.A. as my foundation, my loved ones who are encouraging me to try again and the hand of fellowship that has been extended to me by the very same A.A. members whom I failed. I know that I will and can begin again. No more excuses, nor looking for someone to lay the blame on, just plain honesty is going to work now.

The first night back here was the hardest night that I have ever had in prison. Lying on my bed, I began to take "inventory" and ask myself "Why?" I knew (but didn't want to admit it to myself) I was a phony when I went out of here trying to "bull" myself through the various A.A. groups and, as a result, it backfired on me. The tragic part of the whole thing is that not only am *I* a

victim of my foolishness but there are those who trusted and believed in me who are hurt, too. A broken home, shattered dreams of marriage, children who learned to love me, an employer who gave me that "one chance," the parole officer who bent over backwards to help me, and the good, decent and wonderful friends who fed and clothed me and gave me shelter while I was getting on my feet—those are the ones who are really hurt by all this.

This time, it *has* to work, I must really get with it and make it work! Life is too short and too precious to give it to the state to use in this useless merry-go-round of nothingness that they choose to call "punishment."

Begin again, that is my goal. I never want to "finish" on this program, but I want to be always in the throes of learning, for never in this world or the next will any alcoholic "graduate" in his task of overcoming alcoholism. Certainly this alcoholic won't, as I have so soundly found out. Admission and inventory and a willingness to help yourself, are the keys to success.

S. S., Colo.

One of those bad cons nobody can reach

For me, as for most alcoholics, it was "Eat, drink, and be merry, for tomorrow you die." But, of course, I couldn't die. I painfully awakened each time, mentally, physically, and spiritually sick. Nothing could pull me out of the abyss but more alcohol. Later on, it took alcohol fortified with other drugs to pull me up. Still later, even alcohol and chemicals together could not lift me.

There are many things worse than dying, but is there any death worse than the progressive, self-induced, slow suicide of the practicing alcoholic? The alcoholic suffers death many times over. Alcohol wrings the guts out of life, eats into the brain in such a way as to make the alcoholic blind to the truth. I served twelve years in prison, never suspecting that without alcohol I would not have been in prison at all. Had it not been for A.A. in prison . . . I'll never know, but my educated guess is that I would not be alive today.

You see, I am a five-time loser, which means five felony convictions (not including the cases beaten). I served time in four penitentiaries and several prison camps, including a maximum-security camp during the 1950s. The two years I spent there, I was incorrigible, and the records bear this out. Also, I was insane at times—according to society's yardstick. But when I cracked my leg with a sixteen-pound sledgehammer in the rock hole, I was fighting the system, using my body. Same thing when I let lye and water eat away at four of my toes and my foot for five hours. I was an agitator, a troublemaker, and many men as bitter as I was followed me.

I do not want to digress into the dynamics of penology. However, one thing I am certain of: Inmates in prison who attend A.A. have their chances of remaining free greatly enhanced—this is a proved fact. Of course, an inmate must begin living the A.A. way "inside," if he is to stand a chance "outside." Intake of alcohol changes one's personality—even the healthy personality. If my personality is inadequate, antisocial, or full of kinks and I alter it with alcohol or any chemical, bingo! There go

58

my good intentions, fear of consequences, will to care, responsibility for my behavior. What else can I do except what I have always done in the past?—act as my old self and return to prison. It is estimated that two-thirds of the men in prison were under the influence of alcohol and/or drugs when they committed their offenses.

Yet prisoners often can't identify with many A.A. members' drinking stories. Well, this is understandable. Most of us did not stay out of prison long enough to run the alcoholic gamut—to develop the ongoing kind of alcoholism or alcoholic drinking you hear about in A.A.

We always, or nearly always, had good intentions when we were released from prison. But with the first drink, our good intentions dissolved; our personalities changed. We reverted to the old way of life we knew—a life full of anger, vindictiveness, resentment, fear, dependence, denial, self-will, irresponsibility. And we found ourselves back in prison, where our personalities became even more warped.

Sobriety and a plan for living that produces a personality change and a spiritual awakening are imperative. Through A.A., many receive the needed change and awakening just by trying to live by A.A. principles and associating with A.A. people. We do this by going to many A.A. meetings with an open mind and a desire to live the good-feeling life without chemicals—liquid or otherwise.

Through A.A., we can experience freedom from self. After all, it was self (you, me) that stood in our own way, that ran the show and ran ourselves into bankruptcy, that hurt the ones we loved. All Twelve Steps of A.A. are designed to kill the old self (deflate the old ego) and build a new, free self.

I would rather talk about the good things A.A. has taught me; I feel that hitting on just a few sordid points should be sufficient to let those of you in institutions know where I came from.

In 1953, in a prison in my native state, I spent eleven months in solitary confinement, bouncing in and out of the "hole" (a bare concrete-and-steel cubicle) about five times during those eleven months. Each ten-day period in the dark hole, I was fed bread and water daily, with one full meal on the third day only. I thought that was bad until I hit the hole at a prison camp; it was just wide enough and long enough to lie down in. There, I received several soda crackers and water daily, and before I could have my third-day meal (again the *only* meal in ten days), I had to drink a glass of castor oil or mineral oil, depending on the cruelty of the person who was doing the dispensing. Ten days of this treatment the first time knocked me from 200 pounds to 130, and I seldom stayed out of the hole long enough to gain back my weight.

I wore stripes and chains. Shackles were permanently affixed to my ankles. There is really nothing to dressing with chains and shackles on, once you learn the technique of pulling inside-out pants through the shackles.

I was one of those bad cons nobody can reach. The first time I remember seeing or hearing of A.A. was in 1956. They were having a large A.A. meeting in the prison auditorium. (Two large red A's stand out in my memory.) In those days, I trusted no churchgoer, and thought A.A. was for weaklings. I didn't even try to understand. I didn't know I was an alcoholic and (like most men in prison today) could not relate alcohol to any of my past troubles.

I was taken to my first A.A. meeting out of prison in Los Angeles in 1960. For five years, I was in and out of A.A. in Los Angeles, Phoenix, and San Francisco. In 1965, I threw away all my A.A. books and decided never to return to A.A. I was living, but I was dead.

In 1968, I left California and came back to my native state. I had been in several hospitals for alcoholism. Then I committed my last offense. Three weeks after an armed robbery in which one person received a superficial flesh wound (I could have killed someone!), I was apprehended. I woke up in jail, sick, withdrawing from alcohol and speed, already a four-time loser, and now with a fifth felony charge against me. This was the end of my world, November 13, 1969.

Fortunately, I received only fifteen-twenty years, and I went back to my alma mater (where I had spent so much time in the hole) in February 1970. I was forty-four years old; my life had been wasted. I sank into total despair. I hit my bottom. However, I still would not attend A.A. in prison. I nearly reverted to my old, incorrigible self— had trouble with a couple of other prisoners, was planning an escape. If I failed, they would throw away the key, and I would never get out again.

Then the miracle happened. While I was taking inventory in the cold-storage locker one Sunday in July 1970, a wooden sign bolted to the inside door stopped me dead in my tracks. It was the Serenity Prayer! The words jumped out at me. I suddenly remembered one of my first A.A. meetings, where I heard, "If you are alcoholic and if you continue to drink, the end is death or insanity." They hadn't mentioned the living hell before death.

Yes, I knew what the Serenity Prayer was—A.A. had taught me. It was to be my lifesaver—the final catalyst. (I am looking at it now in my bedroom—a copy that was presented to me a couple of years ago by the A.A. group in that same prison.) During the 24 hours after running into the Serenity Prayer, I think I took the first three Steps for the first time. I surrendered totally. I began to sleep, to relax, to accept my plight. I started going to A.A. in prison on July 27, 1970.

When I had served only eighteen months of my sentence, this ex-incorrigible was placed in honor grade. (God works through people.) Shortly thereafter, I was transferred to the honor-grade unit, where I spent the most painful year of my life. It is painful to grow, and without the help of my "civilian" A.A. companion, big Gene, I might not have survived that critical year of adjustment. This A.A. friend took me into his home when he had me out on pass. He and his wife more than accepted me; he listened to all my woes; both of them treated me as a human being.

Shortly thereafter, I was selected, with eight other inmates out of the 10,000 in the state's prisons at that time, to attend a school designed to take former "management problems" like me and convert them into paracounselors. After nine months of training, all the rest of my class was paroled and went to work in the Department of Corrections. I was not eligible for parole, until—with God's help, I'm sure—the governor cut five years off my sentence. I was paroled on October 27, 1972, when I had served less than three years. Then I, too, went to work as a counselor in Corrections. One would have to understand the correctional machinery to see what a miracle this really was.

After a few months there, I went to County Mental Health as an alcoholism worker. Now, I have been an alcoholism counselor for over a year and am off parole. I go back to my old alma mater occasionally to give A.A. talks, and—just think!—the warden is my friend. I count my sobriety date from July 27, 1970, not November 13, 1969, the date of my last drink. Being dry is not being sober.

Three weeks ago, my phone rang, and a voice I hadn't heard in over twenty-three years spoke. It was my ex-wife, and she said my twenty-seven-year-old son, who has completed his Marine Corps training and graduated from college, wanted to see me privately, was getting married in three months, and wanted me at the wedding. I haven't seen my son since he was three and a half years old. He doesn't know me, nor do I know him. I thank God I am to see him this month. At the wedding, I hope I will also get to see my daughter and their mother. My daughter was one and a half years old when I last saw her. I attempted nearly two years ago to make some amends and contact my children, but it wasn't God's time yet.

Nothing that has happened to me do I deserve. I'm talking about the good things that have happened. I owe everything to A.A. and God. I take credit for nothing. I will be fifty years old next month, haven't seen my son or daughter yet, nor my daughter's two children, my grandchildren; but I am grateful. It is all like a dream. Life is such a mystery, but the mystery is becoming beautiful.

Forgive me—I cannot write further about this latest turn of events, anticipating seeing the family I deserted so long ago. Besides, I can only live today. I must be

ready and willing should I never see them. This is difficult, but it is the only way it has worked for me.

I am still arrogant, egocentric, self-righteous, with no
humility, even phony at times, but I'm trying to be a
better person and help my fellowman. Guess I'll never be
a saint, but whatever I am, I want to be sober and in
A.A. The word "alcoholic" does not turn me off any
more; in fact, it is music to my ears when it applies
to me.

God bless all you people in A.A. and especially you
fellows in prison. Remember, now you have a choice.

Anonymous

From the inside out

"Why A.A. in prison?" I have often heard asked. "You
can't get anything to drink in there anyway." Though
perhaps surprising to some folks, alcohol *can* be acquired
in prison. And if for some reason it can't, many alcoholics will turn to other drugs that *are* readily available. On the other side of the coin, though, many people
first hear about the program in prison. Outside prison
they seldom cared enough to listen. I know. I am a
prisoner.

I came to prison in 1967 as a parole violator. Having
previously served almost five years for armed robbery
and kidnapping, I had not changed my self-destructive
attitudes or drinking habits; and during that period, I
never once heard of A.A. It's likely that I was not ready

to listen anyway. Sure I drank heavily, but a problem? Not me. All my problems were caused by relatives, wife, circumstances—you know, the world had never been fair to me, never given me that "big break."

In 1968 I received a death sentence. Then on a detainer in 1970, I received a second death sentence. I lived on "Death Row" for four years until my sentences were changed to life imprisonment. During that time I did not care about anything or anyone. Like dead wood in a forest, my attitude reflected doom, extinction, and decay. I moved only when prodded.

In the winter of 1971 I was suddenly mainstreamed into the general prison population. My attitude improved a little, but the reminder that I would never leave prison again slapped down my wobbly hopes. So why care at all? I "made time" by creeping through tasks and chores just to make existence bearable for myself. But this didn't work either. Finally in 1974 a "drugged-up" prisoner shattered my snail's pace. This "divine intervention" began my awakening.

Like a rubber band the prisoner snapped a blade against my jugular vein. My blood shot out to all points of the compass. I thought I was going to die this time. My old attitudes, my past life, my future dreams all seemed a sham in that moment. I saw how phony I had been all my life. But immediate intervention occurred so I didn't die, and thus I began my solemn search for something to which I could honestly dedicate myself.

In the spring of 1975 I was moved to another part of the prison where the A.A. recovery program flourished like a refreshing green forest. But I was under the impression that A.A. was a religious program.

A friend who knew that part of my problem was alcohol-related persuaded me to attend a meeting. I agreed on one condition: If I did not like the meeting, I would not go back. I was determined not to be preached to.

The first meeting was confusion for me: all the slogans, the reading of the Preamble, How It Works, talk of taking the Steps. But I paid attention to an older, white-haired fellow named "Dale." He was talking about God, higher power, love, and fellowship. "Ha, just as I expected. Religious types," I muttered to myself and made up my mind not to go back.

But I noticed Dale also talked about not drinking, about how our attitudes, isolation, problems, and drinking were all tied together. I did not know that after several years of working with A.A. in prison, Dale was wise to the reluctance of prisoners like myself. After that meeting, he made a point to welcome me, shake my hand and say, "We are glad to have you. If drinking was a problem for you, this is the place to learn how to do something about it. We *care* about you and will offer all the support we can if *you* want to quit and stay sober."

As I left the meeting, Dale's declaration and show of concern lingered in my thoughts. I needed to learn more, so I returned for the next meeting. A guest speaker arrived and told his story. Some of his points hit home.

I did not become an instant A.A. convert, but I kept going to meetings; and I went back twice a week for eight years. During this time I became involved with service work for the group. Slowly and subtly I became liberated, absolved, delivered from my destructive ways and obsessive thinking about the past, the present, and the future. I began to focus on one day at a time. I feel I underwent the "personality change" spoken about in the program. I still feel surprise and elation today when people sometimes remark on how much I have changed for the better—and this makes my recovery stronger. We all need a pat on the back now and then.

Through ten years—1975 to 1985—I feel that I have branched out, like a rejuvenated tree. During this time the A.A. recovery program has taught me that I cannot control or handle alcohol—or any drugs—so my best bet is to leave them all strictly alone. I have learned how to resist "that urge."

During these recovery years, alcohol and drugs have been available—they always are. Even in a maximum security prison someone tried to sell me two pints of bonded whiskey after I had been in A.A. a couple of years. For me, this was an immediate temptation. I could almost taste it. But I did not buy it. Without A.A. I would have been unable to resist. With A.A. I stood out of danger, though I curiously asked, "Why did you bring this to me?"

He replied, "I figured you were one of those 'alcoholics' and you might want it."

Needless to say, he wanted a high price, too. I explained to him that A.A. had convinced me not to drink. Then I sent him away and my first close call was successfully resisted.

One of the strongest attractions of A.A. in prison is the outsiders who bring in the message of hope and recovery by telling their own stories. Each of these speakers probably has a more "interesting" place to go, but each chooses to come inside a prison to hold out the hand of A.A. These speakers—sincere, honest, and friendly— always seem glad to be at prison A.A. meetings, reminding the prisoners, "Many of us could be drunk, dead, insane, or in prison ourselves." Some bring literature, many radiate spirituality. Their loyal friendship has given added inspiration to the recovering alcoholic in prison. Several of these speakers are former inmates who found A.A. "inside." Now they are bringing the A.A. message back to others. They have inspired me to make plans to do the same some day. Yes, with recovery hope has returned a part of my life I thought lost forever.

For two years at other institutions, I had no A.A. group. But a recent move has given me the close sharing and caring of A.A. meetings again. But here at this facility we do not have regular outside speakers. We are currently working to encourage A.A. people to come "inside" to share with us.

If anyone asks you to share the A.A. message "inside," you may well find such service meaningful, liberating, rewarding, and honorable. Your story and your help is a Twelfth Step call that really counts if you befriend and inspire just one of us to stay sober, to get out and remain out. Does Alcoholics Anonymous work in prison? Definitely.

D.A. Maury, N.C.

'You weren't arrested—
you were rescued'

I'm writing this from a prison, in which I am serving a two-year sentence. When I first arrived here, I guess I was like so many other inmates—I had a lot of mixed feelings, and I was blaming everybody else for my being here.

After I had been here for a couple of weeks, I discovered some A.A. pamphlets. And after answering about fifteen questions in one of them, I discovered I was an alcoholic, among other things. I say "other things," because I was also a very emotionally disturbed person, and now I know most alcoholics are.

Prior to coming in here, I spent a year and a half in and out of mental institutions. Each time I entered one, I was asked if I had a drinking problem, and of course, my answer was no. So, upon leaving, I was just as sick as I was when I entered. The only difference was, I had some pills to "cope" with my situation.

When I entered the A.A. program, I was on the bottom, and I mean *really* on the bottom. I had to accept the Twelve Steps program—either that or go out of here in a pine box. I had had twelve suicide attempts in two years.

I was raised in a good Christian home, so I was no stranger to a Higher Power. My only problem at first was, I started to run away from that Higher Power. Oh, my excuse for running away was my parents, but as I look at it now, it was really that Higher Power.

I started drinking at the age of fourteen and progressively drank more as I got older, and my problems grew with it. Because of drinking, I lost my wife, a business, and job after job. I also lost a lot of friends.

Like every other alcoholic, I couldn't see past my nose. In fact, I couldn't stay sober enough to see my nose, let alone past it. It was always somebody else's fault that this or that happened. The walls of resentment, hate, self-pity, selfishness, and all the other emotions attached to alcoholism were higher than the prison walls that now surround me.

One of the lifers in here said, "You know, Don, you weren't arrested—you were rescued." And oh, how true that is! I'm not too pleased that I'm in here, but I'm really happy and thankful A.A. was here.

I guess—in fact, I know—that the Step for me was Step Nine. It was also the hardest Step. But for me, it was the key Step to a whole new life. I got rid of all the guilt, and boy, what a relief!

I know I have a lot of problems to face. One of the biggest is going to be getting respect back upon leaving here. But I know, if I live and walk through life with the A.A. program, I will surely succeed. I have to work very hard on the Twelve Steps in here. Our problems are basically the same inside these walls as they are outside. We're still alcoholics, whether we're dry or wet.

The biggest reward of the whole program for me is the Twelfth Step. The program gave me back, not only my sanity, but also the God I had been running from all my life. I did have a spiritual awakening, and what a blessing! I learned the truth about myself, plus the truth of what life is about.

D. R., Westminster, B.C.

My name is Tom

I had a happy childhood until I was fifteen. Then alcohol got the best of my father. One night while I was sitting in the kitchen, eating, my father stuck a double-barreled shotgun, loaded, under my throat and backed me up against the wall. A few months later, while he was intoxicated, he woke me up in the middle of the night. He was standing over me, ready to hit me with an ax. I didn't know what was wrong with him. All I could think about was getting away from home. I wanted no part of my father, I had nothing but hate for him.

When I was sixteen, I went to a Citizens' Military Training Camp for a month and I fell in love with that way of life. I decided then to enlist in the Army when I was eighteen and make a career of it. Shortly after, I was at a friend's house one evening, and we were mixing chemicals in a bowl. One of the fellows threw in a match and it exploded, burning me from my shoulders up. I lost my eyesight and all my hair, and was in the hospital for quite a while. Home again, I would lie on my bed in the dark, unable to see, and my father would come up at night and on Saturdays and Sundays and curse me up and down. He told me that I would never amount to anything, never be good for anything. How I hated this man!

About nine months later I got a little sight back in my left eye and, although no sight has ever returned to my right eye, in a matter of a few days the vision in my left eye was completely restored. My hopes soared, perhaps I could get into the service after all. When I was eighteen I got the necessary papers and put them on the table in front of my father. He threw them on the floor. He would do nothing for me. Five months later my mother finally signed the papers. To his dying day my father never let her forget what she had done, and beat her many times for it.

I was worried, knowing that you couldn't get into the Army with one eye. So, for the first time in my life I cheated. I memorized the chart when I read it with my left eye, and when they covered my good eye I just called off the letters I had memorized. I got in the Army and had a wonderful life for about two years. I got very friendly with an Italian-American boy, even got to writing his family. At Christmastime we would get packages from them, and this felt good. He was like a brother.

Then we went overseas. On our second invasion I was sent out on a patrol, and my pal, Tony, volunteered along with a few others. We went as far as we were supposed to, trying to contact a Canadian paratroop outfit. We were returning into our own area when our company commander jumped up and hollered, "Shoot them, shoot them, shoot the dirty bastards." Our men opened fire and killed everybody in the patrol except myself.

The last words I remember of that time were the words of my buddy, who said, "Tommy, Tommy, help me." And I could do nothing but stand there and watch him die.

I went all to pieces after that. I refused to do anything for my C. O. All my hate came back, all the hate I had inside of me.

A Board of Officers told me I had to get to work. I said, "All right, give me a job where I can be all alone. I want no part of you people." They gave me a job operating a bulldozer. We were on K rations and I saw better food going to other outfits, so I decided to get myself a crate of good food. I hooked onto a trailer at the harbor and took off. When I got up in the mountains I pulled back the tarpaulin on the front of the trailer but all I could see was Scotch whisky. I pulled back the tarp at the other end—more Scotch. I had a whole trailer of whisky! I took a bottle out, opened it up, and there at the age of twenty-one I took the first drink of my life. I liked what it did to me; it eased all the pain inside, and all the hurt.

I dug a hole with the bulldozer and buried the trailer-load of whisky. During the next months I drank it all—except some that I gave to fellows in another division when they were leaving, and then they got blamed for stealing the trailer.

Without even knowing it, I became the same man that my father was, the same drunkard, the same wild man. I was so alone in myself that I would speak to no one.

When we returned to the States I was given a twenty-one day furlough. I took thirty, and was arrested, drunk. When I got back to camp, I went under the fence, over the fence—took any way to get to town and get liquor. I got into a fight with the men, I hit an officer, I was court-martialed, fined and shanghaied out of my outfit. I would do nothing but drink.

I volunteered to go back overseas. I hit Europe on D-plus-30 and went all over, hitting the cellars to get wine or whatever I could. And I remained alone.

When the war in Europe was over I signed for the China-Burma-India caper and was waiting for a ship when the war ended and I had to return to the States. I immediately re-enlisted for six years and again I cheated to get in. I was given a ninety-day furlough and I didn't even get home. I didn't even complete the ninety days. I was arrested, drunk, and brought back to camp, to be sent to Korea, but asked if I could be sent to the islands. I wanted so much to go there to get to where my buddy was buried. I had made a promise to my pal when I was drunk. I would go to his grave, look up and say, "Don't worry, Tony, I'll get them for you." But I never did, because I was given a physical in Alaska and couldn't pass the eye test so I was discharged. They had finally caught up with me. From Seattle, it took me six weeks to get home, drunk all the way.

My first job after the Army was working on the natural-gas pipeline. Three of us came late one day and the foreman swore at me and I hit him with a two-by-four. I got nine months in the county jail and it didn't even bother me. I had hatred and the desire to cause damage.

Out of jail, I went to work dynamiting. The fellow I worked with drank too, and we put too much dynamite in the hole one day and knocked out windows half a mile away, so I had to quit.

Then I really hit bottom. A judge sentenced me to up to ten years in prison. He said to me, "You are no good to society or yourself." And I didn't care. When I walked through those big doors into prison, I called it the Big House of Hate, and that's exactly where I belonged because I was loaded with hate.

I didn't stop drinking in prison. I got a job in the bakery where we made our own pruno. And the only thing that kept me from flipping when all the hate and bitterness came over me was going out in the yard and lifting weights. After fifteen months the Classification Board sent me to the farm. There was landscaping to be done and they could use my bulldozer experience. I remember the minister saying, "Tom, you have an alcoholic problem; when you get to the farm, look into A.A." I liked the way he put it. He suggested it, he didn't *tell* me to go.

The day before I was to leave for the farm I was in the mess hall when a fellow tapped me on the shoulder. He asked me if I had a brother in S——; I said yes. He asked if my brother had a nine-year-old daughter and again I said yes. He said, "Well, he doesn't any more. She was killed by a car yesterday afternoon, run over by a drunk driver." That's how they break news to you in jail. I went to the bakery, filled my jar with pruno and got drunk. I asked God why he took the life of a little girl instead of a bum like me. I couldn't understand it, so I drank pruno and just sat there.

I said, "If the guy who ran her down comes here, I'll kill him!"

Monday morning I went to the farm with a big head, and on Thursday night I went to my first A.A. meeting. Three speakers came from the outside. I heard the first speaker, but nothing after that, nothing after Barney. Back in my room I sat down and said, "Boy, *you* feel sorry for yourself. What about Barney? Not only an alcoholic problem, but he is practically blind. You at least have one eye perfect." I went to every A.A. meeting after that.

Eight or nine months later I was coming in from work one day when a couple of fellows said, "Hey, Tom, that guy's here." I knew who they meant—the man who had killed my niece. I didn't go to my room. I went to the building where the new men come, and I could feel goose pimples all over my body, and my hair going up the back of my neck. I didn't know what was going to happen or what I was going to do.

I walked into the big room where the new men were. I had never seen that man before, but I could pick him out. He was standing at the other end of the room. I walked up to him, I called his name, and he turned around and he looked at me. And I don't know what happened to me, but when I looked into this man's eyes I saw all his pain and bewilderment, and I could do nothing but stick out my hand and say, "John, welcome to the farm." We became friends.

I got very active in A.A. and I volunteered for group therapy. When it was completed, a psychiatrist said, "Tom, do you know what you've been doing all these years? You've been running away. You're going to be up for parole soon. If you make it, get into A.A.—and I mean right in the middle. If you just get on the edges, you won't make it and you'll be right back here."

I made parole. And I can tell you that if I hadn't made that A.A. meeting and heard Barney, they would not even have let me out—not if I was still the way I was when I went into prison.

I came home thinking I wouldn't be accepted in A.A. because I had a record, but this was not so. The first night, I remember walking up the church stairs, stopping at the door and thinking, "What if those people inside won't accept me? Should I go in or go back home?"

I grabbed the doorknob and went in. Just inside the door a fellow said, "Hey, Tom, where have you been?" He hadn't seen me in twenty-five years! The second man to shake my hand had been in the Army with me more than twenty-five years before. What a wonderful feeling that was. I couldn't believe it.

For the next three months I made A.A. meetings every night. It's been a whole new way of life. I've never seen such love and such wonderful people, and I shall always feel that the man who started me on this new way of life was Barney, a man who has given so much to the fellows inside prisons.

I have no education beyond the third year of high school, but I know I have a diploma, because thanks to Barney and A.A., I have graduated from the School of Hard Knocks. My goal now is to do a lot of institution work, not to tell my story, but to tell men in jail that they will be accepted in A.A. as I have been accepted.

T. M., Conn.

Shadows have faces

Some 2300 years ago a Greek thinker wrote a parable, *The Image Of The Cave.* He compared men with prisoners chained in a cave, their backs to the light, mistaking shadows on the wall before them for reality. Since Plato's time, writers have allegorized prisoners as "men in the shadows." This is false imagery in the case of alcoholics—we were chained, our back to the light, mistaking shadows for reality long before our inability to grasp reality brought us to prison.

I not only found freedom from shackles of resentment, egotism, and prejudice in prison, but I also learned that the shadows I pursued so futilely in alcoholic search of love, recognition, and belonging are but lifeless projections of the real men and women who await eagerly to give me the reality of brotherhood of which the shadows are but unrealistic distortions—to give it to me warm with the breath of life and pulsing with their heartbeats.

For three years and nine months I have been a ward of the California Department of Corrections as a convicted felon. No wide-eyed first offender I: this is my fourth prison term. I entered San Quentin a recidivist with a "rap sheet" that made hope for a parole a shadow of a shadow. The past, the present, the future congealed, clotting the artery of life and draining the heart of hope. Full of hate for all men, I saw only hatred for me in society's eyes, and I told myself: "T. W., you're dead. You haven't got a ghost of a chance." But I'd once been a lawyer, and I sharpened my weapon of retaliation. I'd be a "stir-mouthpiece" and release men on legal technicalities. It was a crushing affront to find that California courts look rather to the whole to see if substantial justice has been done. Mine was the helplessness of the trapped animal with no claws, no fangs, no cleverness.

When a man is stripped to his naked soul, he is ashamed and fearful before God. I began an age-old prayer, one that self-betrayed men have said ever since the world began: "God, unless you lift me from this pit I've dug, I shall perish." There was no conversion—just the inarticulate prayer of a man who had reached his lowest level.

But things were happening in the pit. I was evaluated by sociologists and psychologists. "You're an alcoholic; you should get into Alcoholics Anonymous." For what? I was bitter. I couldn't get a drink. "You should take a correspondence course in short story writing." That was "the most unkindest cut of all"—I had tried to write fiction in other prisons, but my characters never had any life in them. This advice was some subtle form of torture that replaced the whip and clubs of the other prisons.

But my wordless prayer to God became articulate. I now prayed: "Endow me with the gift of writing." But I didn't write; I was not going to be hurt, be rejected again. Then one day it dawned on me that California would not spend money to make a fool out of a skidrow bum—I was already the world's biggest fool! So I took the short story course (paid for by the Department of Corrections); I got into A.A.; I went back into my Church; I got into group therapy. I was even one of the lucky ones who got a year of intensive psychotherapy. I began to see that alcoholism is but a symptom of an emotional disease; I began to sell stories . . . not all at once, mind you—God is careful in remodeling His clay. A brittle fool has to shed a few bitter tears to moisten him for recasting. Over a period of time it happened.

Three years and nine months it took. Now, I'm going out on parole.

During the past two years I have sold one western action novel to a hardback publisher; twenty-four short stories to religious magazines. I have proof that God, as we understand Him, answers prayers.

The shackles? They've been beaten into tools for building a new life. The resentments are sublimated; the egotism replaced with the real Ego—the "I Am" who is God as I understand Him; the prejudices fade when we realize that everyone and everything is part of God's plan. To change it would be to replace His will with my own.

I even like prison officials. I haven't said "bull" or "screw" for more than a year now. Through empathy I see that, in his official acts, he is far more lenient, more merciful, more just than I have ever been with my fellow men. I actually hope to become as big spiritually as some officials I know. For the man who can lead the blind to light, unstayed by the hate his help initially arouses, is to be big spiritually. And it finally penetrated my thick skull that, were it not for emphatic prison officials, there would be no paroles for recidivists! The average man in the street has not learned, through trial and error, to look beyond my "rap sheet" and initial snarls to see my potential for good. . . .

So I go out soon now. The shadows that used to fill my groping hands with nothingness are behind me. I'm walking toward the light. There are thousands of men and women in A.A. who are real—whose breath and hearts are mine on an exchange basis. I just walk up, offer them me, and in this joyous mart of barter there is sobriety and sanity—love, recognition, and a sense of belonging.

That's what it means to get out of prison—whatever the barriers are between any alcoholic and love. For these walls are but symbols of stone piled upon stone by our own selfish hands to shut out others from our true selves. With the Help of God as we understand Him, the walls fall flat—like those of Jericho. I look forward to taking this message to others and helping them out of the shadows of unreality into the bright sunlight where shadows have faces . . . *friendly* faces.

T.W., Los Padres, Calif.

Heed the warning!
—a prison returnee's plea

Probably the most abrupt realization that the oft-repeated warning to attend meetings faithfully cannot be taken lightly comes to men returning to prison. It is the writer's hope that such will never be your experience. Men who have had A.A. experience, either in prison or out, or some of both, and who fail on parole or come back with new commitments, have considerable advantage over men who have failed for the same reason, but who are seemingly unwilling to admit it. The A.A. "returnee" has had forcibly hammered home again that he is powerless over alcohol. His ego is unmercifully wounded, yet on the asset side he has a kit of tools before him to begin immediately the process of rebuilding his life. The Twelve Steps are ever at arm's reach.

My own particular case is not unlike dozens, perhaps hundreds, of others. It was not until I thought I had thoroughly *mastered* A.A., that I knew all there was to know about it, that attending meetings became unimportant. It was a very simple matter to shirk the responsibility of a Twelfth Step call. To make a long story short, I'll omit the monotonous details and take you with me to the wedding reception where I knew perfectly well that "I can take a little—and then leave it alone." My halo had been pinching hell out of me for a considerable time anyway. It is the simplest of matters to stay out of bars these days, however, for this little gem of illiteracy is originating from what Winchell recently tabbed, "the luxury of an American prison."

Cry on your shoulder I will not; there is not a single resentment toward anyone. I'm convinced that everything happens for the best, and the path I had so unwisely started down could certainly have led to a more grave situation. As it appears now, all I have to do is go back to where the cable parted and splice solidly to the part that stood the strain.

My principal regret, and I think I'm entitled to one, is that this situation could have been so simply averted by continuing to attend meetings regularly. Oh, yes, I said I wouldn't cry on your shoulder, didn't I?

Here I think it appropriate to recognize the consideration extended by the California Prison Administration to prisoners seeking to find a new way of living through A.A. We are visited by an outside group each week, and you may believe it, these meetings are enthusiastically anticipated by all. Several groups contribute their time and energy to make, in many cases, the long drive here. Often it is with perceptible display of relief that some speaker refers to his near-eligibility to having been one of us. A.A. Grapevines provided by several of these generous groups are a source of information and entertainment to a growing membership here.

Whoever you may be, wherever you may be—if there is one unvariable dictate in A.A. it is: Failure to apportion unreservedly a regular, reasonable amount of time to attendance of meetings, doing Twelfth Step work, and participating in the generally available social activity of one's group is a hazardous procedure. Without fear of contradiction I state that it is *never* safe for a member to curtail his participation entirely.

It is far from my intent to make of this a tear-jerker, and it is not motivated by a preponderance of self-pity; the simple fact is that had I not permitted my thinking to become twisted to the extent that I devaluated A.A.'s importance in my life, I most certainly would not have traded a happy, carefree life for the relative nonentity of being just another number in a sea of them. After more than two years of uninterrupted sobriety in the San Diego area, I stubbed my toe, but good. Be that as it may, I am not discouraged.

I am starting anew with the First Step, and with the help of Ol' Buddy, I'll make it next time. If this sincere disclosure of what, more than any other factor, caused me to fail to make the grade helps just one member to realign his thinking and gives him impetus to clear the ever-imminent obstacle, I will be well compensated for setting it down.

Your Pen Pal,
Folsom Prison, Represa, Calif.

"I will not return to prison as a convict"

The day I walked out of those iron gates of Folsom Prison, I made a promise to myself: "I will not return to prison as a convict."

That night, January 18, 1971, I attended my first A.A. meeting as an "outside" member. When I walked into that meeting in San Francisco, many people came over to me, put their hands out, said, "My name is——," and tried to make me welcome. I don't have to say I was very nervous on my first night on the outside. I met many people who said, "Keep coming back."

Wednesday, January 20, 1971, I got on the plane for Los Angeles. My sponsor and his wife were waiting for me when I arrived. I walked up to him and put my hand in his, and we greeted one another. We picked up my bags and left for greater Los Angeles to talk to my former boss. I went in, and he told me, "I can't hire you this week." But they had promised to hire me the day I got out!

So I went back to the car and said, "I don't have a job." All I had were the clothes on my back and $40.00. And I was scared. But I knew that drinking would only make it worse. So I stayed with my sponsor and his wife. We drove to Pomona, stopped to eat, and then went to their home.

I made phone calls to my parole officer, to let him know I was in town, and to a friend I had once worked for. The friend hired me for $2.00 an hour. That meant I had some money coming in.

That night, we went to the men's group in Pomona. The meeting made me feel great. I could talk freely, and I did. I met a lot of great people, had some good A.A. talks after the meeting. Then my sponsor and another A.A. took me to a hotel to stay.

Thursday, January 21, my sponsor came to the hotel and took me to work. I was paid each day, and that helped.

That night, I went to a meeting in Pomona. My sponsor ran the meeting. He asked if he could give his pitch time to someone who just got out of prison. They said yes. I spoke for about twenty minutes. Everyone liked what I had to say. After the meeting, many people came to talk and shake hands. We got to know one another. Again I felt great.

So this started my A.A. in Southern California. I came out of prison with the thought in my mind to stay out of prison and not to drink. I kept going to meetings, hoping to find a group where I could feel at home. And I did, in the Pomona area.

Now, I tried everything I could to get either a motorcycle or a car to get to work. But I had no money and no credit. And who would sell me a car on $2.00 an hour?

But I did not drink. Drinking would not help. So I didn't worry about it.

Then a friend of mine talked to her boss and told him no one would give me a job, because I just got out of prison. So he said to come in. I did, talked for an hour, and started to work February 1, 1971, for this big company at $2.20 an hour. (By the way, the friend was a member of A.A.) I started by cleaning up the place, and I tried to be the best. After two weeks, my supervisor told me, "Ron, you're a great worker." I got a ten-cent pay increase.

Then a friend of mine helped me to find a beautiful apartment. Strange—in thirty-one years I'd never paid any rent. I'd either lived in a place with others or family, lived off women or men, or whatever, to pay my way. So now I had a new job, my own pad. Man, I felt great! Out from the walls, sober, with many friends. Freedom to go to the meetings I wanted to, go when I wanted, eat what I wanted. It was great.

Then something else happened. A woman sold me a '64 Chevy for $50.00. I went around a corner. A police officer stopped me and gave me a ticket as long as my arm. No taillights, no turn signals, one headlight. So I took the car home. The thing I thought funny at the time was that I had no ill feelings about the ticket. I felt the officer was just doing his job, like I do mine. This itself was honesty, given to me via A.A.

One day, I walked into the top clothing store in Pomona and opened a clothing account.

I kept working! My boss told me I was still doing a good job. I got a job change at a fifty-seven-cent-an-hour increase.

Then one day I got a phone call. It was a girl I had met one night in Reseda. We had spent a lot of time with each other. She called to say she wanted to see me. So I went.

The next great thing—we got married. We had a beautiful wedding. We are very happy.

I still attend meetings in Pomona, Los Angeles, Reseda, Ontario, Chino, and Claremont. I speak whenever I'm asked and do whatever I can to help someone who may go down that same road I did. I feel great going to the meetings with my wife. Also, when we have children, I'll try to apply this program to their lives (if they want it). I'm very sure, as they grow up and see how happy their mother and father are, they'll also want to share their lives with the wonderful and understanding people of this simple but beautiful program.

So here I am today, still sober. I'm still in the program of A.A. I'm still honest. And I'm still happily married.

I now have a '65 T-Bird, fire red (almost paid for). I have all kinds of credit. I have a very understanding and beautiful wife. I live in a better place, a ten-by-fifty-foot mobile home. I also have many, many friends in the program.

Now I understand why *I* never made it before. *I* tried to do it myself. That's why I went back to prison. Now *we,* as a group, can and will make it, with God's help. For this I'm grateful. So I say to all the many people in A.A., thank you! You have given me a new life. Everything that I have is because of A.A.

Thank you for listening to my story—an ex-convict trying to find God and stay sober and honest and close to God.

R. E. L., Pomona, Calif.

Freedom

In the March [1959] Grapevine is an article ("A Good Gripe") by an inmate of the Massachusetts State Prison who brings up that oft-pondered question: Why have A.A. available at institutions where intoxicants are generally not on hand?

While I agree with Ray that drugs—and sometimes booze—can be obtained behind walls, I wonder if, from the alcoholic's standpoint, that isn't a minor hazard. I searched his article in vain for some mention of what I believe to be a greater danger—namely, the mental and emotional jag—available anywhere, anytime. Such has been my experience, anyway, and I wonder if there are others. . . .

In '53 and '54 I served seventeen months in a small western prison where there was no A.A. group . . . no treatment program of any sort . . . and not enough work to keep more than twenty-five percent of the inmate population working. During that confinement I took the attitude that I would solve all of my problems right on the day of my release and settled down to do some plain and fancy daydreaming.

There was nothing to interfere with those cozy speculations and always they revolved around me . . . me . . . me. . . . It turned out to be seventeen months of stagnation. Seventeen months in prison without a drink, but every day I was drunk from the heady wine of my fantasies and emotions.

On my release, the actual conditions in the free world just would not conform to the rosy pictures my inflated ego had conjured up in prison. I started drinking almost immediately—just to take the rough edge off of reality—and after being back with my wife and two children for just four months, I found myself before a judge again . . . forgery again . . . fantasy again.

But that judge knew of the drinking, and of A.A. —in spite of my record he placed me on probation with the admonition to attend at least a few meetings. There followed a whirlwind courtship with A.A. that lasted for just about a year. I stayed sober during that time, primarily (I still believe) on the strength of the fellowship found in the A.A. group. I didn't have much use for those Twelve Steps—they were primarily for the "weak sisters"—but I kept that view to myself because some of the guys put a lot of stock in them.

It would seem that reality and I were destined never to get together. When I left that first group (graduated myself—how else?) I went on only one more drunk . . . but it lasted six months. During the last few weeks of that binge-to-end-them-all, I went on a little tour of the upper midwest with a "travel now—pay later" plan of my own design. The "pay later" part of that trip cost me fourteen months in the Wisconsin Prison, and I am currently paying an installment in a county jail in southern Minnesota. And the end is still not in sight: there are other charges pending.

On arriving at the Wisconsin Prison, however, some strange new doubts had sifted into my thinking. I began to suspect in earnest that life was not proceeding according to plan. Not that there *was* any plan, necessarily; but, well, prison did not seem to fit into any rational design.

Then came fifty-four weeks of psychotherapy and the discovery that there had been very little in my life that was rational. At the same time, our Sunday morning A.A. meetings were starting to take on some new meaning. This potent combination of A.A. and psychotherapy was spoon-feeding me back to reality.

But it was a difficult recovery: I fought it every step of the way, squirming and dodging, always looking for that compromise. In time, though, I came face to face with myself—and what a hell of a mess that was. It was suddenly a difficult proposition just to live with myself. All the rottenness and deceit of the past paraded into consciousness, and having to acknowledge finally that all the heartache of yesterday was my own handiwork began wearing on me. It was this steadily accumulating sense of guilt that finally broke me. One lonely night the remorse was especially acute and in despair I turned to God with the whole mess, helpless, penitent, for perhaps the first time in my life.

All I can remember asking for was strength, mercy, and forgiveness. And God performed His greatest miracle that night. He granted me that forgiveness and renewed me with a strength I never knew existed. I went to bed that night dumbfounded, and slept deeply.

That happened fifteen months ago, and I haven't known a bad day since. The consequences of the past are still with me: I'm still locked up. But the penalty has been removed and contact with my Higher Power has been restored. A strange new peace and quiet emerged from that experience which has never left me. That odd hurt in my chest is gone, as is the restlessness and anxiety.

It's ridiculous to claim freedom in jails and prison, but that's exactly what this is. I've known more freedom—the important kind of liberation—in these past fifteen months than I've seen in the whole of my thirty-two years. There is no more fear or tormenting doubts in my life and I've found the key to fulfillment in such counseling and small service as I can render to my fellow-inmate. How much more like a brother he is since I came out of my shell and found him grappling with essentially the same problems that conquered me!

It would perhaps make a better story if I could report that I had gained my physical freedom as well, though I'm content to leave that in the hands of God. (That fact alone is a miracle of patience for me!) Then too there have been many choice bits of consolation. People are aware of the change and I have new friends working to get my detainers dropped. My sentence here is a tenth of what it should have been. Finally, I heard from my wife for the first time in over a year and, by a miracle of faith, she and the children are waiting for me. I know now what the Psalmist felt when he wrote, "My cup runneth over. . . ."

It would probably make a better A.A. story if I hadn't needed the help of so many other people outside of A.A. But, psychotherapy, religious counseling, and the encouragement of the many wonderful people at the Wisconsin State Prison, however, all had a hand in this transition from wet to dry. (Behind the ears, that is!) I still marvel at being able to look back on a prison experience and, because of the people involved, have a pleasant remembrance of my stay there.

In therapy, I learned many new truths, got my inventory started and found myself (happily) a beginner in the A.A. program. While it would have irked me to be told so at the time, I nevertheless *did* join our prison A.A. group hoping to impress the parole board. Now, I can no longer kid myself—and so the urge to impress other people is leaving me.

The danger of emotional binges is ever present, but now I recognize them for what they are: the prelude to an actual drunk. There remains for me only one instrument that will effectively guard against both the dry-drunk and the wet-drunk, only one method that approaches the problem from as many angles as there are sides to the human personality—Alcoholics Anonymous. And I join Ray, and the thousands like us, who gratefully acknowledge the tremendous importance of A.A. in prison.

Therapy helped to correct a serious personality disorder, but an inherent character weakness remains: while the mental faculties are getting dried up, the physical plant is still a potential drunkard.

My efforts to spread the good news about A.A. right here in a county jail have given meaning to my present sentence. And one last bit of consolation: a court order has been prepared permitting me to attend an intergroup session to be held in this city, and I'm going to speak to that group. If I tell them nothing else, they are going to hear how the quiet hand of God came into my life, and how I committed my life to Him when His truth made me free. That's God—as I understand Him.

Merv K., New Ulm, Minnesota

Adding up the score

A girl who found A.A. in prison writes her "outside" sponsor a few weeks after her release.

Dear Georgiene:

I am going to write this and clarify it in my mind as I go along. I want to share these thoughts with you. You have just now received your present [an unopened half-pint of whiskey] from me and along with it this letter.

As I write this it is sitting on my dresser along with my hair oil and cologne. It is the same color as my shampoo and it means no more to me than my bottle of shampoo does.

It meant something to me when I bought it. I shook all over inside and out and I got that terrific pressure in my head again. I looked around outside the drugstore to see if anybody had observed me. I felt so guilty that if a cop had tried to arrest me for breaking the law I would have gone along and willingly pleaded guilty. Of course, buying a bottle on Saturday night is not against the law of the land. But it is against the "A.A. law" and it is not God's will that I get drunk; it is against your principles and mine.

I bought it to prove something to myself. If I drank it I wanted to know how it would affect me. Would I have the DTs? Would I stay at home or go prowling? Would I get my novel out of my locked suitcase—I haven't read it or worked on it for months—or would I come down to your apartment and say, "Well, what do you think of me now? You are always telling me what a nice person I am and how much faith you have in me . . . what do you think of this?" Would I cry for Joe? Would I go to the bowling alley and look for Kenny? Would I ever be able to stop?

If I did not drink it I wanted to know why. I am finding out as I write it down on this paper. I left it lying wrapped up and on the bed for fifteen minutes. I ignored it and fooled around straightening up my closet. Then I took it out of the sack, sat down on the chair and stared at it and read the label. I thought: "Why, this little so-and-so! How could I let a little old bottle of liquid run me and my life? It is nothing. I am something. I am a human being and on the way to becoming a pretty darned good one. This bottle has power to make sniveling cowards out of people. I can go it one better and beat it at its own game. I could go out right now and give those same people the knowledge and the power never to drink it again as long as they live. I am the master here and I say to hell with you."

I got up and set it on the dresser. I turned on the over-head lamp and let it shine full in my face. I looked in the mirror a long time. I saw the strain I had been under for the past week—the 'flu and fever I'd had, my swelled sinus—but, I saw a lot more. I saw eyes that were bright and clear and looked out at the world with good will and kindness. I saw that the friendship of the A.A. members had made a great difference in the expression on that face and that the mouth looked like it might be able to grin at any time. It used to be so grim and hard.

I sat down in a chair and added up the score, the personal score. It goes like this:

1. Georgiene B. gave me more than sponsorship. She gave me her friendship. She didn't have to but she did it because she likes me, believes in me and really cares.

2. Elline M. is proud of me and makes it a point to talk to me at the meetings. She invited me to her daughter's wedding. That is the best compliment I have ever had. I'll go, too.

3. Rosemary D. and I are forming a fine friendship.

4. Dean B. says keep up the good work and shakes my hand.

5. Charlie M. says I've "got A.A."

6. Alex V. singles me out to encourage me at meetings and really likes me.

7. Margaret B. offered to share her home with me.

8. John H. enjoys my company.

9. Fran W. and Gene R. will be my friends as time marches on.

10. I have the opportunity to make a dream of Georgiene's come true. This should be No. 2 blessing on this

list. I can go back to the Indiana Women's Prison as a speaker, sponsor and example and help the girls and help make up to Georgiene for all the grief and heartaches she has endured the last three years.

11. I was made head waitress after three weeks on my job. I am doing good work there.

12. I work hard and on my one day off a week I got up early and went to Champaign, Illinois to try and help Janie B.

13. I have attended three, four and five meetings a week and six different A.A. groups in order to get the message as soon as possible so I can be a good working member and give back what I have received.

14. I have found out what Christian love is between people. Bishop Sheen talks about it all the time but I couldn't believe in such a thing. Now I know.

15. I have taken the first seven of the Twelve Steps and I am letting God have His way with my life. He is doing a pretty good job.

16. I am happy in one room. My happiness has little to do with what I own.

This is the list of the best things that have happened to me in the thirty-one days since my release from prison. How could I expect or handle any more than I have at this time?

Before I started this letter I walked over to the closet to get my pajamas. All of a sudden I said, "Father, watch over me. Help me to do as You want me to do."

Georgiene, He did.

Your friend,
Dorothy
Indianapolis, Indiana

No longer a phony

Two words kept jumping out at me every time I read Chapter Five in the Big Book: "rigorous honesty." I could understand what was meant by the simple fact that to succeed in this program, an individual must be honest with himself. But why this "rigorous" business thrown in? As a matter of fact, honesty is referred to *three* times on the first page of Chapter Five.

As I kept trying to work the program and tried working that Fourth Step, I finally realized why the honesty portion is stressed with such force. Without it, no Step and no part of the program can be worked with any degree of success.

To relate the effect this has had in my life, I'd like to share an experience with other inmates who are in A.A. or contemplating joining a group. No matter what an inmate's position or status is in prison, an unwritten "code of ethics" is constantly influencing everyday decisions. Hardly a day passes in prison (or in the free world) when a person isn't confronted with a choice of being honest or not.

I work here as a draftsman and architectural estimator. I have access to just about any kind of technical illustration and art supplies. Needing to find some means of support, I decided to set up a greeting-card hobby for profit. What better position could I be in for a venture of this nature? One of the reasons I chose this particular hobby was the fact that I would have almost a monopoly on the business. I could purchase a few low-cost supplies to cover my art card, which is required of us who want to work an art hobby in the cell. The rest could be secured from the state while I was on the job.

Why not? They could surely afford it. I rationalized that I did a good job for them all day, five days a week, so why shouldn't I "borrow" a few of their supplies? At approximately the same time, I got "political" in the A.A. program here (I was phony as a three-dollar bill at this point) and managed to hustle enough support and votes to win the secretary's spot.

This is the point when the monkey wrench really got thrown into the old machinery. As the big shot of one of the largest A.A. groups in the Texas Department of Corrections, I decided to start reading some of the literature and books about the program. I didn't want to be embarrassed by not being able to snap an answer right back to any questions that might be asked of me.

Well, most of you A.A.s know the rest of the story—I got hooked on the program! I fought with my inner self day and night. Here I was on Sundays in front of 200-plus inmates telling them that A.A. was an honest program, and I couldn't get honest with myself yet. I can't put my finger on just exactly when it hit me, but when it did, I unloaded every piece of contraband I had in my house (that's my cell, for those of you who don't know what I mean). We sometimes refer to getting rid of that heavy load we carry on our shoulders. Well, I can assure each one of you I became 10,000 pounds lighter at the moment of truth.

Naturally, I wanted to go out and tell the world all about it. I went to three or four of my close associates connected with the A.A. program here and told them about what had happened and how great it felt. No one in prison accepts things at face value, and I feel quite sure most of those I told were thinking this was a phase I was going through. Knowing what a phony I had been, I sure couldn't blame them.

I don't know whether this was my spiritual awakening, but I do know that my life has definitely changed for the better. As a result of whatever it was, I now am more pleased with myself and others, and I work the program more "rigorously" than ever before.

In closing, I might say to any newcomers to prison A.A. programs that the meat of the program is in the Alcoholics Anonymous Big Book. Instead of just sitting on the fringes of the program, pick this book up and read it from cover to cover. You'll be glad you did.

Stan, Texas

Suddenly the program came alive

I have been around A.A. for about nine years now. I don't remember the circumstances surrounding my first meeting, but I do know that I had a problem with booze.

At age fifteen, booze meant so much to me that when my high school sweetheart threw my bottle out the car window, I hopped out to get it. I didn't stop to think that we were on an expressway and traveling about fifty miles an hour. I paid for this particular bottle with a broken leg, a concussion, and a six-month convalescence. I didn't think at the time that my bottle really had anything to do with what was happening in my life. Now, I can see that my problems, as well as my drinking, were getting progressively worse.

I was only thirteen when I started drinking. At fifteen, it was already taking a heavy toll on me physically. At sixteen, I started getting in trouble with the local police. I was known as a nice kid. But when I drank, I was known as a kid with a problem, to say the least.

I seldom sat at home and was out in gin mills daily and in strange places at weird hours. For example, if I had an urge for some egg drop soup at 2:00 AM, I would find myself in the neighborhood Chinese restaurant's kitchen, cooking. More often than not, I would also be found by the police, bleeding from cuts I had suffered from walking through the restaurant's glass window or door. The police call this breaking and entering. Another habit I had, if I needed a drink and the bars were closed, was to smash the window of a liquor store and help myself to a bottle or two. The police called this burglary.

After about six arrests, the courts felt it was time that I did time. I was sentenced to three years in an upstate New York prison. When I arrived at this state institution, I saw a lot of the same people that I had hung around with in my neighborhood. It didn't register with me that I had a very narrow circle of friends.

While in prison, I did my thing and drank daily. I had a good job, which afforded me the opportunity to make as much jailhouse booze as I would need to do my time. I did two years of my sentence and came out no wiser than when I went in.

Somehow, I found out about A.A. and figured I would give it a shot. The people I met at the meeting were really nice. I liked what they had to say and the way they said it. However, I was not ready to throw in the towel. I felt I had a few more good times left. For the next few years, I bounced in and out of A.A. like a rubber ball. When I was hurting, I would go to A.A. and get dry and use to my advantage the parts of the program I liked. When things started looking brighter, I would leave my friends in the program, forget all I might have learned, and go out again and get hurt some more. Then I would come crawling back asking for help.

There were always people at A.A. willing to help. I did not want to help myself, though. Not 100 percent, anyway. I would take part of the program, and the rest I would do my way. I hit quite a few hospitals and did quite a few short stints in jail during this time in and out of the program. I went to school and acquired a good position in the medical field. But I didn't like to stay at any one job for too long, because I didn't want people to figure out my drinking patterns.

I would get involved in my community, as well as my job, during these spurts of dryness. I had a very good position with a political party and was a delegate for a national union. But when it was time, I would go out and blow it all by drinking. I did not feel worthy of any of the prestige or credit that went along with the positions I held. I didn't know myself that well, and what I did see in myself I didn't like, so I went back to my bottle.

Now the blackouts were more frequent. I woke up on Miami Beach with a hangover and sunstroke, and I didn't even remember leaving New York.

I came to the conclusion that I was nuts, and that's why A.A. wasn't working for me. The people in the program were nice, and I wanted to be one of them, but I found that I was not capable of being honest. I went on like this for eight years, with a dozen more arrests, last rites half a dozen times, the loss of a few cars and jobs, and a three-week marriage. Eight years went by after I left prison, and I woke up standing before a judge who sent me right back to an upstate prison. I saw my whole life flash by while I was standing before that judge. I was sent to Sing Sing and would lie in my cell at night trying to figure out where I went wrong. After a couple of weeks there, I was sent to a place nicknamed "Little Siberia," the prison farthest from New York and my home.

This was the place where I learned about sobriety. I had a lot of time to get to know myself. I really thought that I wasn't a bad guy—in fact, when I didn't drink, was a pretty nice guy.

I went to the A.A. meeting there and was disheartened. I saw about ten guys telling jokes and having a good time. I talked to the group chairman and asked him what was happening. He told me that the guys just didn't feel a part of A.A. They were in a joint and couldn't drink anyway. I asked him if I could share with the guys.

That night, when I spoke, A.A. had such a different meaning to me. All of a sudden, the whole program made sense. It was like someone else was talking inside of me. What came out even surprised me. The guys apparently liked what I had to say, too, because at the next meeting, I was elected group chairman. Because I got involved, a few of my friends in the joint gave it a shot, too. More and more inmates were getting involved. We started a treasury. We elected a program chairman, a G.S.R. (general service representative), and a secretary. The more people who took an active part in the program, the more we grew. Some A.A. friends from Canada started coming to help us in our meetings.

The group grew from ten people once a week to seventy people twice a week. We got into Step meetings and the Traditions. There were a lot of outside A.A. people who helped with literature and moral support. Our members, maybe for the first time in their lives, knew what it felt like to be a real part of something. Something good and beautiful, at that.

Last February, we had our first group anniversary, with some 200 people present. The guys in the group really put a lot of work into our anniversary. I also celebrated my first anniversary on that day. I felt something that day that I had never felt before. It was something that I can't explain; I can only say it was electric. I was sober for one year then. I could honestly say that I liked what I saw in myself. For the first time in my life, I was grateful to be alive, with the power to think and plan, with the knowledge of what life is all about, with the capacity to love and be loved. The sharing displayed by everybody present at that meeting is something that I never want to forget. When things are bleak, I can always reach into my memory bank to that day and gather strength from what was present throughout the affair.

I left the prison last month and now am in a work release program near home. I go to work five days a week. I go to A.A. at night. Each weekend, I go home and stay with my loved ones. I can appreciate the people that I love today. I get up in the morning and thank my Higher Power. I have a toll-free number to Him today, and I can call and not only ask Him to help me, but say thanks, too.

I like being sober. I like being a part of A.A. I am grateful that I was given another shot at what A.A. has to offer. I know what being grateful means. I will always feel a part of that A.A. group upstate in prison. It took the unselfish sharing of a bunch of cons to teach me, and for that I am grateful, too. I hope some day to return there and share with some others who might be less fortunate. I know that in order to stay sober, I have to share it. I can't think of a better way than to give it back to the people in our prisons, for they played a very important part in my life.

Thanks, A.A.; thanks, God; thanks, all the A.A.s in all our prisons.

R. M., East Meadow, N.Y.

Inside and outside

I am an inmate of a state prison and a member of Alcoholics Anonymous. We refer to our members here as "inside" and to all A.A.s who are not in institutions as "outside" members. In my mind, those terms have another meaning: the "inside" and "outside" of me. The outside is the obvious, that which others see and hear; the inside is that which only I know—my thoughts, feelings, fears, frustrations, and anxieties, as well as my hopes, faith, desires, and ambitions. This, I am sure, is true of all of us.

I am thirty-five years old, and this is my second experience with A.A. inside a penal institution. I will not attempt to include here all the misery and the unrewarding escapades I have had throughout my drinking career. I will say, however, that it began when I was very young, about nine. By the time I was fifteen, I was well on my way toward being a qualified alcoholic! Of course, I didn't know it then, nor did I find it out until several years later.

I guess I was a very typical alcoholic: terribly egocentric, with perfectionist ambitions, but never quite living up to my "standards." I have an above-average IQ (whether that's good or bad), but I quit school after graduating from the ninth grade. I was fifteen then, and I was already a member of the Colorado National Guard. Because of the fighting in Korea, my unit was activated and sent to Texas for training and preparation for duty in the Far East. Fortunately, my mother interceded, which led to a minority discharge for me.

From that time until I was twenty-six, I pursued just about every goal under the sun, both in regard to employment and in my drinking habits—the former mainly to provide for the latter. I was married twice and divorced twice. Then I awoke one day to find myself incarcerated in "the world's largest walled prison," in Michigan. (Oh yes, I did everything in a big way!) It was there that I first came into contact with A.A. and learned how serious and degrading my drinking problem had become. I began attending A.A. meetings in the prison partly out of frustration, partly out of curiosity, and partly because attendance was strongly recommended by the prison officials. In fact, when the judge had sentenced me to two to fourteen years there for forgery, he had said it was more to dry me out and straighten out my thinking than for punishment. But, regardless of why I began attending the meetings, I soon found something I could grab hold of. To this drowning man, A.A. was my straw of hope. I became quite active in the group until I was paroled, about fifteen months later.

Since I was (I thought) sincere about my sobriety, and since "no drinking" was part of my parole stipulation, I continued my association with A.A. for about a year after I returned to society. Then, as my pride and my ego were rebuilt, I began to feel that I hadn't really been a desperate alcoholic—I just hadn't learned how to control and pace my drinking. By then, I was climbing the ladder to the stars in radio and television broadcasting. Who ever heard of a star who couldn't drink? It was socially essential, I was convinced—and, above all, important for my ego!

Well, that settled the matter. I would keep my drinking under control. Somehow, I got away with it for nearly five years. I remarried my second wife, became a father, and made myself quite well-known in my profession. These achievements were followed by another divorce, a lost job, and another prison sentence. I will be here for not less than one and not more than ten years. The charge: unlawful use of credit cards. Believe me, this is not the easy-payment plan!

We say alcoholism is a progressive disease. I have learned that A.A. offers progressive recovery—that is, if we really want it. And I do. It has become the most important aspect of my life, now and for my future. I am currently the secretary of our "inside" A.A. group, and I know for the first time that I am really "inside" the A.A. program, spiritually, mentally, and morally. "Spiritual awakening" would be an inadequate description of my renewed relationship and communication with God as I understand Him. I don't despair that it took so long; I just thank Him every day that I have found the way.

I was born four days after the inception of Alcoholics Anonymous. Thank God for both events. I look forward with joyous anticipation to being able to join with A.A. on the "outside." At this writing, with the grace of God, it may be possible within the next few months.

R. P., Carson City, Nev.

Living free

The time was 0700, and it was April Fool's Day, 1977. I was dressed in civilian clothes, my own clothes, which I hadn't worn for a long time. From the window in the stone building of the reception block at Dartmoor Prison, I looked out at the all-too-familiar scenery of the prison grounds—the neatly arranged little flower beds, the cold, shining tarmac of the driveway leading to the prison gates. The moment had come for my release.

Unlike many who have known this same emotional prize, I knew where I was going, where the road I would tread was leading, what the future held in store for me. It was in the right hands, because I had been for the past two years a member of A.A. Because I am an alcoholic.

There were four other inmates released with me. We were driven to the railway station in Plymouth, handed our respective rail warrants, and left to catch our train.

Once on the train, after buying smokes, coffee, and so on, we settled down in a compartment to enjoy the sheer ecstasy of our newfound freedom. About 1000 [o'clock], three of our party made a beeline for the restaurant car, where there was a bar. They returned shortly afterward, loaded with booze. They had found their goal. This had been the dream uppermost in their minds during incarceration. By the time the train pulled into Bristol, there were three drunken and rather unsavory ex-convicts, ready to take on the whole world. They were it! They were managing directors of the universe. They were free —and completely irrational and irresponsible, to say nothing of the two heads they had grown en route.

I observed this without comment, but with a feeling of sadness. This, I thought, was the reason so many of us were destined to return to prison within a short period of time. This was what I myself had done on other occasions when released from prisons. But not this time. I had at last found a means to change all that negative insanity, to grow up. Slowly but positively, I was experiencing the kind of change that happens in A.A., the necessary change that we alcoholics undergo if we are to lead normal lives.

I was free, but only to the extent that I was released from bondage. My real freedom had come long before, when I was still locked in a cell. At the moment, an old poem had come to mind and had been seen in its true perspective: "Stone walls do not a prison make,/Nor iron bars a cage." I thought how true this was for me. An alcoholic is a prisoner of alcoholism locked within his own private hell.

I had decided I would not try to play it my way this time. I would not try to play God. For once, I had learned how to listen and to take advice from those who had the same problem as my own. I knew from bitter past experience the futility of being my own master, of going on this false, pride-filled ego trip. I had tried many times and always failed, and each failure had been progressively worse. I had lost good jobs, given up good jobs, and lost two wives, three lovely children, two homes, a business, and my character. I had landed in mental hospitals and prisons, in ever-worsening circumstances. I knew now why these things had happened to me. "Why me?" and "Poor me!" were no longer options for me. I had become willing to listen, to respond in positive, constructive ways, to remain always teachable.

Life hasn't been all roses and honey since my release. I've had my share of ups and downs, of coping with problems. There have been some job problems, for example. Right after release, I worked as a self-employed electrician, with my own small business, but it didn't pay well. When I found myself in debt after six months, I decided to pack it up and get out of the trade, to get a secure job working for someone else.

I tried for some time to find a worthwhile job to settle into. When I eventually did, I was sacked on the fourth day, after talking with the managing director and telling him the truth about myself. It was just one more case of misunderstanding, plus the fear that having an ex-convict working in a key position might have damaging effects on the business if customers discovered the facts about my past.

Through the A.A. program, I was able to accept such a setback without self-pity or anxiety. The fact that things haven't gone as smoothly as I'd like hasn't thrown me off balance. I accept whatever comes—a far cry from the old Mike of the drinking days! The job situation has begun to look up, with work in hand to last about a year, further contracts in sight, and some long-range possibilities. I know that even if present opportunities don't work out, something will turn up sooner or later.

My wife and I have settled down happily to our new life together, and she is very grateful to A.A. for what it has given me. I get to meetings regularly and have made many good friends, and I try to carry the message that was handed down to me.

The amazing thing is, when problems come along, I can cope! I can be responsible and face up to the problems. I can recognize my faults and defects and when they crop up, can work on changing them. I have to work the program all the time, every day. When I catch myself thinking the way the old me used to think, I have to switch off and replace that old thinking with positive, honest A.A. thinking. This works, one day at a time.

I don't even want a drink any more. Life is different now; it has purpose. Life is working the A.A. program, going to meetings, learning how to grow up and stop the insane habit of landing in prisons and mental hospitals. The choice was mine—to change—and the choice is ours to make, today.

M. B., Ledbury, England

A 'real bad' alcoholic

At the age of thirty, I knew I was an alcoholic, but it took another ten years to find the way to the front door of A.A. Only the real bad alcoholics had to go to A.A. After six months of daily meetings, I knew I, too, was one of those "real bad" alcoholics.

In those first meetings, eighteen months ago, there was a man who had a saying, "They told me when I came that A.A. has a wrench to fit every nut that walks through the door." That seemed humorous at the time, but it couldn't apply to me. Today, I'm grateful there's a wrench to fit every nut that walks through the door, because I sure need a wrench to fit me.

Nine years in the seminary, followed by twenty years of daily church attendance while I was building a seemingly prosperous business, made me a tough nut to crack. Sure, I was an alcoholic, but not such a bad case.

110

Hadn't I quit drinking seven years before coming to A.A.? It didn't seem worth mentioning that in the meantime I had learned how to get drunk on pills.

The Twelve Steps are the key to getting that wrench to work right. If the Steps won't do the job, nothing ever will. I have tried enough other programs of recovery—spiritual, psychiatric, Oriental, mystical, and just plain commonsensical—to know they don't work for me. A.A. is the last resort for someone who has finally reached the desperation of a drowning man.

Early on in A.A., I thought I had a dual problem, alcohol and drugs. After so many years without a drink, the drink problem seemed to be solved. It took a while to realize that a handful of pills had the same effect as liquor—oblivion. One day, it dawned on me: The pills had been a substitute for alcohol. It was ridiculous to come out of a three-day blackout from tranquilizers and pain pills to pat myself on the back because I hadn't taken a drink—at least, as far as anyone could tell. There were no empty booze bottles.

As long as I accept in my innermost heart that I can never again drink as normal men drink, I know I belong in A.A. and must apply the Steps daily in order to live without alcohol. I cannot use *any* drug or medication that affects my mind or my emotions. Such drugs and medications will lead me back to alcohol and death or insanity. My reprieve is just for today, and only if I maintain my spiritual condition.

That is not easy. I used to be an "expert" on spirituality. Today, I am like a confused child, trying to learn about true spirituality. In the first four Steps, I have come to see how I deceived myself into thinking I had a strong belief in God. People who believe in God don't do the things I did. Today, all I can do about spirituality is go to meetings and read the Big Book and try to take the Steps and ask God for help. The rest is up to Him.

Before A.A., I used to boast about being an alcoholic who had quit drinking. One day, I bragged to someone who was in A.A. He dismissed my feat casually by saying, "Oh, you're just a dry drunk." That was no compliment. Soon, my friend zeroed in with an invitation to a meeting. I went as a favor to him, or so I thought. For the next seventeen months, it was one meeting or more nearly every day.

All the disasters that have taken place since that first meeting were ready to happen. It was as though I had made a snowball high on a hill, and during the last eighteen months, I have watched it grow and grow as it rolled slowly down the hill to crush me. There were times when it seemed the snowball might melt or roll off to the side, but it didn't. Today, I'm glad it didn't. There may have been no other way for me to learn what I needed to learn. Perhaps the final crushing blow has come, and I have hit my bottom at last.

My problems are of my own making. One of the high points of my life is the day I began to understand that phrase from the Big Book. Knowing my problems are of my own making helps me to accept with some peace of mind the consequences of my own actions.

I am still finding out how sick I am. That discovery process has been frightfully painful, but I am grateful for it. There is no chance at recovery till a person sees how badly he needs recovery, and how hopeless it is for him to try to recover on his own.

At the beginning, people used to say, "Keep coming back. Things will get better." I kept coming back, and things have gotten better, but not in the way I thought they would. I am definitely not more successful in all areas of my life, as I thought I would be. When I came to A.A., I had a fine job, a lovely, sophisticated wife, a new $10,000 automobile, and a charming place to live. After a year of sobriety, I was without wife, job, car, or money, and was saddled with a hopeless pile of unpaid debts. As if that was not enough, after seventeen months of sobriety, as a result of certain actions before coming to A.A., I became a guest of the United States Government as an inmate in the psychiatric unit of a maximum-security Federal penitentiary. All of this had to happen for me to see how hopeless I am without the minute-by-minute help from a Higher Power.

Are things better for me today? I didn't have to drink today. I have hope. There is light at the end of the tunnel, though it sometimes is faint. When that light dims, there are all those sober drunks in A.A. They are living, breathing proof that things do get better for those who work the Steps and are willing to wait.

J. M., Corpus Christi, Tex.

My name is Helen

My name is Helen, and I am an alcoholic. Like most of us, I found A.A. the hard way. I knew that I had a serious drinking problem a year before I had to do something about it. A man was dead, and I had a second-degree murder charge facing me.

At first I thought, "Well, it's too late now. Why not drink myself to death?" I had tried to die several times already—why not now? By the grace of God, I am alive today. It must have been His will, because living certainly was not my will.

The only reason I wanted to be released on bail was so I could get to another bottle of sleeping pills and another bottle of Scotch—and this time I would have "the good sense" not to call anyone for help.

My lawyer sensed my sorry state of mind and notified my sisters, and when I was released on bond, a sister was there to make sure I did not harm myself. I went to New York City to live with her until my lawyer decided what to do. She has the same problem with alcohol that I do, and at that time, neither of us would admit it. We began to have vicious family fights. Soon, I was willing to spend my time of waiting in jail, rather than there with her.

Instead, I found my own apartment. This time alone was a godsend. I was still drinking, but without extra pressures, I drank considerably less. I spent the next few months thinking about myself and wondering why I was where I was. I had always been very active in my community and had been highly respected until I met a man, a heavy drinker, and started really hitting the booze. I blamed everything on that unhappy affair.

I went back to Florida in July to begin working on my case with my lawyer. The man I had been involved with was dead, and I was in very serious trouble. My lawyer sent me to a psychiatrist. The first time I saw my shrink, he told me that I was an alcoholic. I went home and drank to that. Another time, he told me that no man could have done all those things to me—I had *let* him do them! Everywhere I turned, I was losing my excuses. I had to face the fact that I alone was responsible. That was hard. Every session was capped with another drink.

Why should I quit drinking? I would darn sure have to quit drinking when I was in prison, so why fight it now? Every time I got smashed, I wanted to down another bottle of sleeping pills. But I would remember the tears streaming down my son's face the last time I overdosed. And I remembered how my daughter went to live with her father because she was tired of the misery at home.

My shrink was patient and always available to me. I think I finally decided to go ahead and quit drinking to make him feel better. I quit three months before my trial, and I found that I could actually face my nightmare better sober. It was still horrible, but at least I could control the urge to kill myself.

Then I began to wonder if it would be feasible to face life (a normal life) without drinking. What would I do at a party? All my friends drank. Well, almost. I had several friends who were nondrinking alcoholics (A.A.s, of course). I was living at the beach at this time, and everyone at the beach was in a party mood. I started drinking tonic and lime without the booze. No one minded at all! I still had a nice time. I still had friends. One more fear dissolved.

I had support from my drinking friends as well as my nondrinking friends. They all cared. For the first time in my life, I began to trust my friends enough to lean on them. And no one turned a cold shoulder. I began to have many long conversations with my A.A. friends, and they were available to me twenty-four hours a day. I finally let one of them talk me into going to a meeting. I really did it to get her off my back. Again, I was surprised at the warmth and compassion I found there—

and some of them even knew I was waiting to go on trial for murder.

I discovered I was the one who had been rejecting people all my life. I began to discover how dishonest I had been with myself and everyone else. I began to discover that people really did like me and that they weren't all after something. Now, I had nothing at all to give but myself.

I was tried and convicted of manslaughter. I am in prison now, and I have been through the usual periods of emotional stress—fear, remorse, hopelessness. Then I joined the prison A.A. group. I found tremendous moral support from the visiting speakers from the outside. But I still smirked when these people assured me that things would get better if I turned my troubles over to God. How in God's name could God help me where I was? He wasn't going to get me out of prison. He wasn't going to hush these eighty women in this dorm at night so I could sleep—or keep them from stealing and swearing and fighting. God may be everywhere, but I surely did not see Him in here!

Then I began to resign myself to my dreadful situation. I continued to go to A.A. and church, hoping for something—not really sure just what. I was skeptical, but the words *sounded* good. And I did begin to feel a little better, and I began to smile occasionally. I even began to feel kindlier toward all these awful animals in here. Then I discovered these "animals" had names—and feelings—and fears—just like me! I began to comfort some of them and worry over them and counsel them, and I forgot about myself for a while. Comforting them comforted me.

One day, I needed to write a letter and mentioned that I was almost out of paper. Suddenly, I had enough paper to write a book. Three or four inmates came to me and gave me sheets of paper from their own supply. I wasn't even looking, and had not seen a friend approach. They had been there knocking at the door, and I had been afraid to answer. I opened the door.

Things are looking up now. My friends in here comfort me, and my friends from the outside do what they can, too. I am learning to live as A.A. has suggested in the Twelve Steps, and it makes life so much better for me and those who live with me.

I am growing in ways that needed growth, and when I leave this place, I will be strong enough to survive. Thanks to God, A.A., church, a wonderful family, and many wonderful friends, I am going to make it now—one day at a time.

H. P., Florida

I try to carry the message back to prisons

My father was an ex-con alcoholic also. When I was only six months old he was shot and killed. I have two older brothers and one sister but I am the only alcoholic and the black sheep.

My mother remarried when I was about eight. I had just finished first grade and my stepfather made me quit school and go to work on the farm. He was cruel to me. I can remember those days as if it were just yesterday. I can remember the times he whipped me so badly that blood would run down my legs and my shirt would stick to my back. I remember the times he knocked me down with his fists.

I just couldn't go on like this. At thirteen I ran away from home—if you could call it a home. Many a night I cried myself to sleep, wanting to see and be with my mother and afraid to go back. Early in life I found that drinking would make me forget my mother and the troubles for a while. How little did I know then what drinking would do to me later. But at the start drinking made me forget everything, and gave me courage to do and feel like a big man, and this I liked.

It wasn't too long before my friend John Barleycorn began to treat me badly also. At fifteen I paid my first fine, for drunkenness and assault with a deadly weapon. Soon I got into more trouble and this time left that state.

Sometime later I heard that my mother was ill and at the point of death. I used to sneak in to see her. When I got to the state line, I would hit the back roads and the byroads. Many times I would be drinking on these trips.

Looking over the past I can truly say that, but for the grace of God, I might have been a killer also, because while drinking I carried a gun on me at all times.

I went through three stages of drinking. At first I drank to forget and to feel important. Then I found that I needed to drink to get going in the morning. Then I had to drink in order to live. Blackouts came and I couldn't remember where I had been, or what I had done. I switched brands of whiskey; I switched jobs; I switched towns; I switched states, and nothing worked. I have been in nine states and I have been in trouble in all of

them. Within one year I was sent to a penitentiary in Virginia and to one in Pennsylvania. It was there I heard of Alcoholics Anonymous for the first time.

At the suggestion of the chaplain and two inmates I decided to look in on this A.A. thing—mainly because I had no place else to go. There was something about those meetings! I began to look forward to them. Little by little I felt different. These A.A. meetings had not only become a part of my life in prison, but they had become a part of me also, so much so that I found myself wanting to get out of the drinking business. I knew better than anyone else what a price I had paid for drinking. And somehow, in my weak alcoholic mind, I believed that this A.A. would work for me as it had worked for others.

I made my time in prison work for me by learning all I could about A.A. and by working on myself. I was like a fighter making a comeback. I was trying hard to run my life, instead of letting the bottle run it for me.

When I left prison on parole, I wasn't looking to get sent back. My sponsor in prison assured me that A.A. would work and I had a kind of a faith. For the first time I was looking on the bright side of life. I had a head start. I knew what I wanted. I wanted sobriety more than anything in the world. As I write this letter over eleven years have passed without a drink. It has not been easy, but I have enjoyed it.

My two great desires are for a sober life and to get the A.A. message to behind bars. How do I stay sober? By trying to help my inmate alcoholic friends learn of a new way of life without alcohol. When we get sober something has to take the place of alcohol in our lives. Why not let A.A. fill and fulfill that part?

What good is A.A. in prison? A.A. is good anywhere, anytime. A.A. was a lifesaver for me and will be for lots of alcoholics in prison, if we will carry the A.A. message to them. My alcoholic friends are in prison for the same reason I was there: they could no longer handle the bottle, the bottle handled them; they had no choice in going to prison, the bottle made the choice for them.

But while in prison they can learn—through A.A.— why they are there, and what to do about their lives. They can learn that they do have a choice after leaving. They don't have to drink, and they don't have to go back to prison. Take it from an old ex-con alcoholic, A.A. will work anytime, anywhere, when the desire to stay sober is greater than the desire to drink. As long as A.A. is in the world, there is hope and help.

My hopes and life are set on trying to help the alcoholics in prisons. What about you?

Carl M., Miami, Fla.

Freedom—behind bars

None of us in A.A. reads headlines
like these without a brief shudder . . .
a fleeting vision of "There but for the Grace of
God" . . . and a moment of gratitude and thanks. Those
of us, that is, who go our daily way free to follow any
road . . . as long as we stay away from just one drink.
But there are many thousands who have found the inner
freedom A.A. offers, whose opportunity to test their A.A.
convictions in a normal world is denied them. For some
the waiting is temporary . . . others must practice
these principles in all of their affairs behind prison walls
—some for years, a few perhaps forever. Joe is one of
those and one of us.

I do not remember how I reached Bellevue—but I remem-
ber the DTs and the awful certainty that I would die if I
stayed . . . I was back in the Bowery and then I had the
strangest desire to get home. I started walking. I dimly
remember passing through Connecticut . . . then Rhode
Island . . . then South Boston . . . then the train

home. I was full of paraldehyde and cheap wine. No food . . . no rest. Then—my favorite bar at home, and two men telling me a woman had been slugged with a bottle and the cops said that I had done it. I passed around my pay slip from the hospital in New York where I had been working, but they were still shy and then I went and dialed the number of the police station and each time lost my nickel. So I walked the mile to the station house to clear myself. That was to be my last free walk. I had forgotten I was a cop slugger, hated and feared in that station house. . . .

I was born in South Boston in 1917. There were five in my family. My father died when I was very young and my mother had to go to work to support us. We were depression kids in every sense of the word. At an early age I became accustomed to hard work and I liked it. I was very strong.

Then came the teens, and the house parties where bootleg booze was the thing. I walked off my first steady job because of alcohol. I started driving ice trucks, coal trucks—anything on wheels.

Then started the arrests for drinking. I became a powerful man—I could lift 620 pounds. When anyone hit me they were hit right back. Due to my steady drinking and record of resisting arrest I became known as a "cop fighter." Often I would have to leave my home area because of altercations with the local constabulary . . . I was not a model citizen.

But I never at any time ever molested or robbed anyone. I worked on farms and ships, built railroads, did construction work, and was even a special nurse —and always the spectre of the bottle pursued me. I knew that I would one day die of it but I did not know how to stop.

And so—on October 20, 1945, I was taken from the court to the jail, held without bail on charges of first degree murder and robbery. . . . The trial lasted nine days and the jury was out for forty-five minutes. They returned with the verdict: *guilty of first degree murder, with a recommendation for clemency.* But, it was explained, clemency was not possible under the law—conviction of murder in the first degree meant death in the electric chair.

So, my boy—here it is! Stand up and show that you might be a drunk but you can die like a man. The clerk read off the verdict and the judge intoned the sentence.

That night I was taken to the State Prison and lodged in a cell in "death row." Sentenced to die for a crime that I had never committed . . . yet thanks to my friend the bottle—I could not prove my contention.

I knew I had an appeal pending but I did not know when. After the first six months the first reversal came, but my lawyer still fought on. Each day thereafter became a hell of uncertainty . . . I had long ago lost all faith in a God who could permit such things. Men? Men had placed me here. Suddenly one day my nerves and courage and hopes faded. I saw my picture in its true perspective.

I was alone, and *I* was not enough, any longer. To be alone is not always bad, if you are sufficient unto yourself. But the black day comes when your tools and tricks and artifices no longer command the situation, and then you know fear—despair and hopelessness sit with you constantly.

I do not know the exact day it became too much, but I distinctly remember begging something—someone—for just five hours' peace . . . a day at a time, *one little court calendar day.* From somewhere, someone—the peace came . . . and it has never wholly left me. I have tried to figure it out and have come to the conclusion that to get this peace, you must be a clean vessel, drained of every emotion—pride, hate, fear, envy—all that might interfere with your reception, save the one that you beg for.

I remained in the death cell for twenty-five months. After I gained the peace I needed I tried to make my day the most important thing in my life. Upon rising I asked "someone" for the peace of the coming day—not the whole day, just the hours between 9:00 am and 3:00 pm, the court day.

One night I found that someone had tucked a copy of the Big Book into my daily reading supply. I read it. I got the idea: drunks are not hopeless creatures, incurable, abandoned by God, scorned by men, but sick people— and they can be helped. Then came the realization: Joe, this is the truth, but it comes too late for you. I also recognized that I was living a kind of A.A., only I was doing it five hours at a time.

Then came a night in late October . . . I heard on the 11:15 news broadcast: the Supreme Court had denied my last appeal. I needed my prayer that night instead of the next morning. Somehow I slept and woke as usual. A few days later I was taken to court and my stay of sentence revoked. I was told I must die within thirty days.

When the day came the prison barber was my only visitor. I wasn't brave . . . I had waited so long I just wanted it over. I smoked and thought. I had written all my letters—one to my mother, one to my lawyer—and there was nothing to do but wait . . . until five o'clock, when I would walk across the prison yard to the little area where the death chair was set up—and then at midnight, as the Chinese say, "Ascend the Dragon."

Suddenly the telephone downstairs jangled . . . the officer came slowly up. He looked at me for a moment and then he said, "Get your things together—you are leaving here. The governor has commuted you." I asked for the shoes I had not worn for over two years and a belt.

I really do not know what I expected to hear at the first A.A. meeting I attended in the prison where I began serving my life sentence—but thinking of those other hours of peace, I wanted more. Sitting through those first few meetings . . . realizing that everything made sense . . . that it works—I got in a little deeper each time. Not all the way, at first—suspicion and distrust grow deep in prison. But each week a little more: the first moral inventory, the Steps, the eventual return to my church (after the initial acknowledgement that God was my Higher Power).

I never understood until A.A. the meaning of "Thy Will be done"—thine, not mine. A.A. has taught me that it is not alone a method by which group therapy can help a man attain sobriety. It is a completely new way of life for those who desire it. I do. A.A. means to me a way of life with real friends, a way to cease beating my head against a glass prison, a chance to return to my God and to live as a man and not as an immature child with a drink-sodden brain.

A.A. is life and hope and all that I want from life. Without it I die and I want to live—for me the only way, the A.A. way.

Joe G., Norfolk, Mass.

THE TWELVE STEPS
OF ALCOHOLICS ANONYMOUS

1. We admitted we were powerless over alcohol—that our lives had become unmanageable.

2. Came to believe that a Power greater than ourselves could restore us to sanity.

3. Made a decision to turn our will and our lives over to the care of God *as we understood Him.*

4. Made a searching and fearless moral inventory of ourselves.

5. Admitted to God, to ourselves and to another human being the exact nature of our wrongs.

6. Were entirely ready to have God remove all these defects of character.

7. Humbly asked Him to remove our shortcomings.

8. Made a list of all persons we had harmed, and became willing to make amends to them all.

9. Made direct amends to such people wherever possible, except when to do so would injure them or others.

10. Continued to take personal inventory and when we were wrong promptly admitted it.

11. Sought through prayer and meditation to improve our conscious contact with God, *as we understood Him,* praying only for knowledge of His will for us and the power to carry that out.

12. Having had a spiritual awakening as the result of these steps, we tried to carry this message to alcoholics, and to practice these principles in all our affairs.

THE TWELVE TRADITIONS
OF ALCOHOLICS ANONYMOUS

1. Our common welfare should come first; personal recovery depends upon A.A. unity.

2. For our group purpose there is but one ultimate authority—a loving God as He may express Himself in our group conscience. Our leaders are but trusted servants; they do not govern.

3. The only requirement for A.A. membership is a desire to stop drinking.

4. Each group should be autonomous except in matters affecting other groups or A.A. as a whole.

5. Each group has but one primary purpose—to carry its message to the alcoholic who still suffers.

6. An A.A. group ought never endorse, finance, or lend the A.A. name to any related facility or outside enterprise, lest problems of money, property, and prestige divert us from our primary purpose.

7. Every A.A. group ought to be fully self-supporting, declining outside conributions.

8. Alcoholics Anonymous should remain forever nonprofessional, but our service centers may employ special workers.

9. A.A., as such, ought never be organized; but we may create service boards or committees directly responsible to those they serve.

10. Alcoholics Anonymous has no opinion on outside issues; hence the A.A. name ought never be drawn into public controversy.

11. Our public relations policy is based on attraction rather than promotion; we need always maintain personal anonymity at the level of press, radio, and films.

12. Anonymity is the spiritual foundation of all our traditions, ever reminding us to place principles before personalities.